# Naughty
## CONFESSIONS FROM THE MEN'S ROOM

DAN THE MAN

**Naughty Confessions From The Men's Room**
Copyright © 2024 by Dan the Man

All rights reserved. No part of this publication may be reproduced, distributed, or transmitted in any form or by any means, including photocopying, recording, or other electronic or mechanical methods, without the prior written permission of the publisher, except in the case brief quotations embodied in critical reviews and other noncommercial uses permitted by copyright law.

ISBN: 978-1639459216 (pb)
ISBN: 978-1639459223 (e)

The views expressed in this book are solely those of the author and do not necessarily reflect the views of the publisher, and the publisher hereby disclaims any responsibility for them.

Writers' Branding
1-888-403-0293
www.writersbranding.com
media@writersbranding.com

# Table of Contents

Preface . . . . . . . . . . . . . . . . . . . . . . . . . . . . . . . . . . . . . . . . . . . . ix

Chapter 1.   A Wild-Ass Rymo Talk! . . . . . . . . . . . . . . . . . . . . . . . .1
Chapter 2.   Shit and More Shit! . . . . . . . . . . . . . . . . . . . . . . . . . .5
Chapter 3.   Mr. Cool the Winner! . . . . . . . . . . . . . . . . . . . . . . . .9
Chapter 4.   A Wild, Crazy Story! . . . . . . . . . . . . . . . . . . . . . . . .15
Chapter 5.   An Unbelievable Story! . . . . . . . . . . . . . . . . . . . . . .19
Chapter 6.   Singing His Jingle! . . . . . . . . . . . . . . . . . . . . . . . . . .23
Chapter 7.   Don't Fucking Freak Out! . . . . . . . . . . . . . . . . . . . .27
Chapter 8.   What the Fuck … Is That? . . . . . . . . . . . . . . . . . . . .31
Chapter 9.   The Pitcher Beer Man! . . . . . . . . . . . . . . . . . . . . . .35
Chapter 10.  What the Hell Is Going On? . . . . . . . . . . . . . . . . . .39
Chapter 11.  Hot Foursome Coming Up! . . . . . . . . . . . . . . . . . .43
Chapter 12.  Hot, Wild, Sex Talk! . . . . . . . . . . . . . . . . . . . . . . . .47
Chapter 13.  Shit, Jive, and Exuberance! . . . . . . . . . . . . . . . . . . .51
Chapter 14.  A Swingers Showcase! . . . . . . . . . . . . . . . . . . . . . .59
Chapter 15.  The Best Prank Ever! . . . . . . . . . . . . . . . . . . . . . . .63
Chapter 16.  Blow-Up Dolls and Sheep! . . . . . . . . . . . . . . . . . . .67
Chapter 17.  Sexy and Naughty! . . . . . . . . . . . . . . . . . . . . . . . . .77
Chapter 18.  Short Mini Stories! . . . . . . . . . . . . . . . . . . . . . . . . .81
Chapter 19.  This Sign Really Messed Their Minds! . . . . . . . . . .89
Chapter 20.  Let's Play Word-for-Word! . . . . . . . . . . . . . . . . . . .97
Chapter 21.  Never Dull Moments at The Urinal! . . . . . . . . . . .103
Chapter 22.  A Wild, Unusual Alumni Party! . . . . . . . . . . . . . .111

The Cast . . . . . . . . . . . . . . . . . . . . . . . . . . . . . . . . . . . . . . . . .119
Appreciation Quotes . . . . . . . . . . . . . . . . . . . . . . . . . . . . . . . .121
Let's Talk . . . . . . . . . . . . . . . . . . . . . . . . . . . . . . . . . . . . . . . .125
My Daily Poem . . . . . . . . . . . . . . . . . . . . . . . . . . . . . . . . . . .127
About the Author . . . . . . . . . . . . . . . . . . . . . . . . . . . . . . . . . .129

# Synopsis of
# NAUGHTY CONFESSIONS FROM THE MEN'S ROOM

****

It's always a great opportunity to be a fly on the bathroom wall, experiencing each conversation, and being a spectator of naughty confessions. These stories are profane, wild, kinky, funny, off-the-wall, erotic, raw, sexy, bad-boy talks and hilarious. These real talks take place at the urinals, at the bathroom door, at each stall, and in the sink areas. They are highly lit at celebrity parties, special events, and other unbelievable parties in Florida nightclubs and mansions.

The author has signed release forms from each main character, enables him to write these naughty confessions. All participants have agreed to use their nicknames or a fictitious name. All the stories are true. You, the reader, will laugh, hysterically!

Each conversation reveals naughty confessions of the participants, their friends, their romance partners, mistresses, strangers, and loved ones. There are stories of pranks, orgies, and one-night stands.

Enjoy this nonfiction collection of naughty reality that takes place in the men's room. There are many unexpected surprises and outrageous conversations. These are stories like no other.

# Acknowledgments

****

Thank you, Joni, my love. I will always cherish you forever. Thank you so much, Shampu, for your exuberance, positive mindset, winning image, and great sense of humor. Through our many winning talks, you've inspired me to write my second book. You're amazing, my friend! And it's always a great pleasure communicating with you @Shampu Sibley on LinkedIn and @shampusibley on Instagram. From one writer to another writer, I am looking forward to your first published book.

Thank you, Jamar. You're an amazing inspiration with powerful, positive vibes! I truly appreciate your presence, my friend. And, also, it's always a tremendous pleasure communicating with you @jamarortiz on Instagram.

Thank you, Matt, for your great conversations. I enjoy all of them. You're amazing, my friend with a positive mindset, awesome vibes, and exuberance! It's always a great pleasure connecting with you @mtolb on Instagram.

Thanks to all the university students in Tampa Bay for your support.

Thank you to each host for the fun mansion and celebrity parties.

Lastly, thank you to all my clients. It's always a fun ride and a blast.

# Preface

**\*\*\*\***

This book is another glimpse into the world of funny, kinky, profane, wild sex stories and off-the-wall conversations I have experienced as a men's room concierge. I bring you naughty, real confessions from the men's restrooms. All of the men have elected to use their nicknames or a fictitious name to protect their identity, which I totally understand. These confessions have taken place in a number of places throughout the state of Florida—exclusive private parties, special events, nightclubs, mansions, and celebrity parties. I pride myself on keeping an open mind in every conversation with everyone I meet.

Note: Each celebrity I've had the pleasure of working with shall remain nameless due to my professional contracts. I truly believe in respect and the preservation of dignity. Celebrities always deserve this as well as my discretion on such personal stories as these. My "Dan the Man Code of Ethics" is always enforced.

For every confession in my book, I have all the necessary release forms signed and approved from each featured customer. The actual dialogue between these unique people and yours truly are all featured in this nonfiction book, which covers events in a number of locations. These conversations are not made up—they are all very real.

**Warning: This book contains profanity and erotic content. If bad-boy words offend you, please do not proceed any further because it may upset the living shit out of you! Then, when you get so fucking upset, in frustration, you may throw this book across the room, and frankly, my book is intended to give you the opportunity to be a fly on the men's restroom wall, to experience each true conversation as though you were there and laughing, hysterically!**

# DAN THE MAN

I will now take you through each chapter in the men's restrooms—the real confessions. Thank you for taking the time to purchase my book and enjoy this funny read.

Dan The Man

# Chapter One
# A WILD-ASS RYMO TALK!

****

### A Private Party in Winter Park

This mansion party was wild and crazy, and the positive vibes were just sensational. You could not expect any more from this beautiful event.

The men's restroom was so cool—huge, plush, and bright, a room with ample seating and its own huge widescreen on which to watch your favorite shows. Porn movies were usually played to arouse the male clients.

And, then you have all the crazy-ass talks, and as always, the unexpected. Hell, it's all in fun.

The sad thing about these amazing parties came toward the end. A lot of the distinguished guests were leaving. There were only a few left to communicate. The fun had to finally come to an end.

### 12:20 a.m.

"Hello, Dan the Man," said Mr. Rymo the Lover. "I am here for the last few minutes, it seems. I've heard great things about you, sir."

I responded with a positive vibe, "Hello, Mr. Rymo the Lover. Thank you for the compliment. It's a great pleasure to meet you."

"Yes! It is a great pleasure to meet the famous concierge."

"Thank you. How has your party experience been so far?"

"You're welcome. It's been just fucking pleasurable," Mr. Rymo the Lover answered with his positive vibe. He then said, "Thank you for the foaming soap and hand towel."

"You're welcome," I said. "That's great that you're having an amazing experience."

"There were a number of the hottest sex games played during this party," Mr. Rymo the Lover said. "I must say, I am extremely happy!"

"I heard that there were some very interesting sex games, and there were absolutely no losers at all."

He responded, "Everyone was a winner with a motherfucking blast of happiness!"

"That's so damn great."

Mr. Rymo the Lover smiled and said, "Yes, one beautiful young blonde blew everyone's load. She had a record thirteen cum blasts in her mouth alone. It turned out to be one crazy fucking orgy, but she was the lone cum sucker. I have to say, she took care of my load and enjoyed every last drop of it. Miss Sluthole the Queen was her name."

"Wow, what a fantasy name. Whoa, that is some kind of confession."

"Yes, it sure is," he said. "I know that she is well known as Miss Sluthole the Queen, a pole dancer with the hottest fucking mouth and the hottest lips—your cock stays hard with her sexy presence."

"Okay, so what was the grand prize?" I asked, laughing.

"If you did not want to shoot your load into her hot mouth, her ass was hungry and wide open. She gave you her personal invitation, and she would say, 'Just plow my tight asshole and make me your naughty slut!'"

"Wow! Now, this is some wild-ass, naughty confession."

"Then the second floor was the same sex venue. It was fucking wild and off-the-fucking chain! The hot oils, leather whips, and the hot fucking sex was unbelievable! The third floor was anything goes—just step in a room. Your entrance was granted with open arms. This party offered you the totally unexpected with the hottest ladies, all eighteen bedrooms were occupied. What a fucking sex show to watch!" Mr. Rymo the Lover said with his big grin.

"I know the guys walking into this restroom were kinda worn out, with their tongues hanging out," I said with a short laugh.

## 12:35 a.m.

He responded, "Yeah, Dan the Man, the only one who is not worn out is Mr. Fucker, a good-looking black dude, six foot ten in height with big-ass muscles and a hung twelve-inch cock, just fucking everybody in front of him! Some guy was taking pics, but I didn't want to be featured in their monthly social called 'The Hottest Men and Women at Hot Orgy Parties.' Mr. Fucker didn't mind—he was a big fucking ham and got his hot-as-fuck cock sucked really well and exploded each damn time! I'd rather be very discreet—I have a wife and a mistress, so it's really too fucking complex for me to get involved in that damn local publicized magazine."

"Yeah, that is some damn twist. I must say, it exceeds so many expectations. Wow!" I said, chuckling.

"It sure does."

Mr. Rymo the Lover exited the bathroom, and then the bathroom door opened quickly.

Two regular customers entered the restroom.

"Hello, Jack the Pirate and Dyno the Twist," I greeted them with a positive vibe. "How's it going?"

"Need to take a leak in the worst way. I'm pussy worn out right now. Need a breather," said Jack the Pirate who was catching his breath.

Dyno the Twist said, "We just need to relax for a few moments."

"I heard all about Miss Sluthole the Queen, the prime hot mouth of the party, along with the tightest ass. All the guys so far are just fucking worn out and zoned out to another planet with all their big-ass smiles."

Jack the Pirate said, "This young thing can suck a cock entirely in her hot mouth and swallow all your cum and smile, then look you right in your eyes and demand you give her another hot load—right now!"

Dyno the Twist added, "I shot my load, and she swallowed every bit of it and said, 'Please come back later, and I will open my tight asshole for you so I can take another hot fucking load!'"

"Guys, the naughty confessions tonight are one after another," I said. "It's fucking unbelievable! And she must be something else—the perfect, wild sex dream!"

Dyno the Twist, responded, "Hell, yeah! She took it extremely well!" Jack the Pirate said, "Thank you so much again for your hospitality. Here's your big tip. We're going back for some more head and ass!"

"Thank you, guys, for the generous tip. Enjoy your fun blow jobs and hot, amazing asses!"

**12:55 a.m.**

Mr. Rymo the Lover once again entered the men's restroom. I said, "Did you meet a new gal? You've got the biggest smile!"

He said, "Yeah, but, fuck … I will tell you, Dan the Man, I am just so fucking worn out, my man. My love pole needs a fucking rest. Her beautiful holes had her fucking motor running at full speed, and it never stopped. Then Mr. Fucker took over. He never, ever stops with his huge, overdrive stick shift which keeps on going … going …"

"The confessions are multiplying like a fire hose," I said. "This party is supposed to be winding down, but I think we are going into sex overtime. Wow!"

Mr. Fucker walked inside the men's room. "This is the best fucking sex party I've ever attended—three hot loads for this entire night! It's been fucking sensational! Yeah, I'm ready for some more hot pussy!"

"There is never a dull moment at any of these parties."

"Hell! We are just getting started!" Mr. Fucker responded with his big-ass grin.

Mr. Fucker slowly walked to the bathroom door, ready to exit, flexing his muscles and ready for another sex encounter.

I said, "Don't stop—continue your great sex drives!"

"I will, my man. Another explosion is coming up!" he said in his deep, mysterious voice with a big-ass grin.

"Have another amazing time. Later."

"Later."

Another round of the hottest sex with so many exuberant horny superstars. This had been a hot sex marathon.

## Chapter Two
# SHIT AND MORE SHIT!

****

### A Hot-Ass Night in Jacksonville Beach

This was a hot mansion party in a beautiful area. It was just getting started with hundreds of positive-minded people. The restroom was outstanding. The decor included black and gray marble and gold urinals. The wash area had gold fixtures, and each gold toilet was equipped with a black push-button feature in case you wanted your ass flushed with sprays of warm water to get rid of your nasty-ass shit. Wow! I mean, talk about how the wealthy live. These gold toilets did everything for you except hand you a drink, serve a very nice meal, and introduce you to a gorgeous lady dressed to kill for you to make passionate love to. Now, that's asking way too damn much! Think about it. The black button feature saved money on toilet paper, and it was so damn amazing that the guys were really getting off on it.

### 11:35 p.m.

My very first customer of the night was dressed in a blazing tan suit and designer cowboy boots. He had a very serious diarrhea problem and said with a stern expression, "I am going to take stall number two. Oh … shit! It's coming fast! Glad I made it to the toilet … oh … the shit is pouring out of my asshole!"

"Okay! Just take your time! I am used to these off-the-wall conversations! This is nothing new!"

He yelled from the stall, "Do you have any anti-diarrheal stuff?" I answered in a high-pitched voice, "I sure do! When you're finished pooping, I will have a couple of tablets for you!"

**11:42 p.m.**

A few minutes passed. He continued flushing the toilet a number of times and making some really weird-ass noises.

In a high-pitched voice, I said, "Is everything okay in there?"

"Yeah, I am going to try that warm water spray up my ass!" he belted out in his loud, powerful voice. "What are the towels for?" he asked, loudly again.

I answered, also loudly, "They are for wiping your butt after you're done with the warm water sprays!"

"And, the baby powder is for what?" he asked, loudly.

I answered, just as loudly, "To powder your butt after you towel dry!"

"Man, these rich bitches think of everything!" he said, laughing loudly.

"It's the professional touch!" I responded with a loud chuckle.

Then another customer arrived at the urinal. "This party has so many fine, great fucking-ass bitches!" he said. "I definitely need to get laid tonight. I am due for some nice, tasty pussy because I've had a frustrating week at my high-pressure, motherfucking job!"

"You're in the right place to release all those frustrations."

"Thank you so much for understanding," he said to me.

"Believe me, I do understand. Just have a great time. I'm sure that one of the gorgeous baby dolls will help you anytime. And, you will walk out of here with the biggest smile of pleasure."

**11:47 p.m.**

The guy in stall number two said, "Oh, yeah, that warm water feels great up my ass, and I am getting a fucking erection! Oh … fuck! Yeah, man!"

"Keep your erection to yourself!" The guy at the urinal asked, "Is there a special toilet that really cleans your ass and gives you a real hard erection?"

I answered, "All seven stalls have the black push-button feature to clean your butt after you have taken your shit. I personally don't know about his so-called erection. That is really none of my business. Thank goodness his stall door is closed."

"Now, I think I will go to one of stalls because now I have to take a big-ass, nasty shit. My stomach is about to bust with my fucking explosion!" he said in his serious tone and demeanor.

### 11:56 p.m.

He went to stall number seven to release his shit explosion. Well, it stunk like a skunk. I sprayed and sprayed with air-freshener and sprayed again. Man, did I spray. Wow!

He said from stall number seven in a high-pitched voice, "Yeah, it's been something like ... oh ... my last shit was ... uh, ten days ago!"

"Oh, my! That's way too damn long! I know you will be in the stall for a while! Just take your time! No one is hurrying you! Wow!"

The word was spreading around very quickly about the high-powered, fancy-ass cleaning feature in the stalls. You know, it's really amazing how many guys take shits at these parties. It's through the roof, and each night it happens a record number of times. This is why I always have at least three cans of air-freshener. I would hate for the customers to wear a gas mask because of the horrible shit smell that would eventually knock them out on the floor. Oh, now we have a TKO.

### 12:05 a.m.

The guy from stall number two finally came out with the biggest smile and said, "That was the best feeling I have had in a dozen years, having warm water spraying up my ass!"

I proceeded to say, "I sure as hell would not know, but I am glad that you had an enjoyable experience."

At the same time, the guy in stall number seven said, "Holy shit, that warm water is fucking amazing! It feels so damn great, and now my ass is so damn clean, its time to use these soft-hand towels for a nice wipe! Then, I'll powder my ass really good! Then, I need to settle down my cock! It's standing straight up in the air and really being fucking naughty!"

I said, laughing loudly, "We really didn't need to know about your erection!"

**12:20 a.m.**

Another gentleman walked in and asked, "Hey, I heard you had the push-button erection at each stall. Is this true?"

I answered, "Oh, my. Allow me to explain the black button feature."

As a professional concierge, I hear a lot. Both men were pleased with their positive results from the warm water sprays located in each stall and my professional customer service at the sink area. I am always humored, and of course, laugh a lot at these off-the-wall conversations. It would continue to be a very interesting night. These guys in attendance were on another fucking planet, just raving about these gold toilets and the warm water sprays. It should be a night to always remember—so damn fucking amazing with the cleanest asses in town.

# Chapter Three
# MR. COOL THE WINNER!

****

**A Private Mansion Party in Orlando**

This elite party of the coolest people was talked about for many days before it happened. I was notified by text four days before the party. It read, "Dan the Man, its show time at O1-69, Thu morning, same discreet LOC-169." I responded by texting each time, "OKAY-COPY69." Both are standard text codes. I had become well known, just like the famous professional clients in attendance. Everyone respected his or her individual code at all times.

It was time for the party of the year at a beautiful site, a luxury setting, and a magnificent gathering of many horny, driven people. I looked forward to the hundreds of naughty confessions.

**1:10 a.m.**

A brief description of a well known person.

Mr. Cool the Winner always looked great. His presentation included striking green contacts that were amazing, awesome dreadlocks, and gold grills that stood out to perfection. He was dressed in loose shorts, bright-red tank top, and striking sandals. He was very smooth, cool, and confident. He stood tall at six foot six and had a positive mind-set of exuberance, a winning image, and was determined to take command of the stage as the grand winner.

Now ... back to the party.

This party was off-the-fucking chain—a big celebration, and all of the bartenders were serving straight shots of liquor.

A writer on a popular cable network show said, "Let's all celebrate my ten years in television! Cheers to everyone! Yeah, cheers!"

The loud voices echoed, "Cheers! Cheers!"

**1:20 a.m.**

Guys were coming in and out of the men's restroom stone drunk. This mansion was buzzing with really fucked-up people. There was no stopping, and when they were ready to leave the party, their vehicles awaited them with their own personal sober drivers. Yes, that definitely made fucking sense!

The well known person now enters the men's restroom.

"Hello, Mr. Cool the Winner. How are you?" I said with a happy grin.

Mr. Cool the Winner responded, "Dan the Man, great to see you again, my man. I feel so fucking amazing!"

"It's always great to see you with your winning smile, and I always feel your positive vibes, my friend. You are a grand winner!" I said with a chuckle.

"Thank you, my best-restroom-attendant-and-neat-as-fuck cool guy!" Mr. Cool the Winner responded.

I asked him, "How's the party?"

Mr. Cool the Winner answered, "A lot of winners out there making their rounds. There's hot fucking sex all over this mansion, my man."

"Wow, I know you're going to tell me a number of confession stories about this party," I said, laughing.

He laughed as well and said, "Yes, sir, my man, things are really hopping on the first floor. People don't have much clothing right now, indulging in some grab-ass play. On the second floor, everyone is nude, and they're licking, tasting, and fucking. And, the third floor is kicking ass with one big fucking orgy. The leather slings are a hot conversation topic right now."

I responded, laughing, "Wow, Mr. Cool the Winner, yeah, I'd say that this is going to be another big, amazing, wild, nude-ass fucking celebration."

"All the bars are occupied with so many fine young ladies, fully nude. They are taste testing and eating their delicious pussy pie deserts," Mr. Cool said, maintaining his cool image.

I responded, "Oh, my, very tasty and many to eat, I bet." He said, "Yes, sir, my man. On the first floor, both bars are full of the finest, legs up in the air, lying on the bar. It's party time! These guys and the beautiful young ladies are having their delightful snacks, delicious, hot, tasty pussy for everyone to enjoy. Boom with my fist pump!"

"Whoa, back at you with my fist pump! Let's blow it up, my friend!"

### 1:30 a.m.

"On the third floor, there are six leather sling stations with chains, handcuffs, playful whips, and hot lotions," Mr. Cool the Winner said, chuckling.

I responded, "These are amazing setups for some really hot-as-hell sex."

"Hell, yeah! There is enough for everyone to enjoy. If you didn't get a hot-ass bitch, then you did not attempt to get a great piece of ass and some of the tastiest pussy around this planet! You don't belong here! Boom with my fist pump! Yeah! Fucking boom with another fist pump, my incredible man!"

"Boom, my fist pump! Wow! This is so hot!" I said with my exuberance.

"Let's explode it again with my big boom fist pump, my cool-as-fuck friend!"

"Hell, yeah, Mr. Cool!"

At this time, a few guys came into the restroom with only a shower towel wrapped around them. One guy mentioned they had just completed another hot sex session and needed to take a piss badly.

Mr. Cool the Winner said, "You guys really got some kind of a great cardio sex workout."

A guy from the recent sex session said, "Yeah, it was so fucking amazing with a hot foursome!"

I said, "That's so cool. It sounds as if they are all amazing—never a bad session."

"Dan, I just got a text. In the next few minutes, the slings will be occupied by six hot new bitches, and yours truly is invited to participate. My man, it's only for those with huge cocks! It's the exclusive big-cock club! It's time to unload my motherfucking load again!" he said with a big-ass smile and his positive, winning vibe.

I said, "Mr. Cool, go for it. The elevator outside the bathroom door just opened for your invitation."

"Later, my man."

About an hour and a half passed. The restroom was really quiet because of the wild sex parties taking place on all three floors. I was just being patient. Then from a short distance, I heard a few loud voices. It wouldn't be long before my customers arrived back in the men's restroom.

Five minutes later . . .

**3:05 a.m.**

A few guys entered the restroom with only bath towels wrapped around their middles, but Mr. Cool the Winner walked in completely nude. He absolutely got expressions of many stunned looks! I kept an open mind, but was totally shocked on his wild freak show entrance.

"Mr. Cool the Winner, you've got to cover that spitting anaconda of yours. Damn, you're still dripping!" Everyone, laughing loudly.

Mr. Q from the security team walked in and said, "Wow! Mr. Cool, you got to cover it up, it's the bathroom policy, not a porn show!"

Mr. Cool the Winner responded in a low, exhausted voice, "Thanks, Mr. Q. I have a bad habit of exhibiting my BBC beauty."

"No problem, just cover it up!"

I said, "Thank you, Mr. Q for your assistance."

He responded, "Always my pleasure, Dan."

Mr. Cool, here is a good-sized bath towel," I said, continuing to laugh, loudly.

He said in a soft voice, "I appreciate the towel. My snake is all covered, my man."

Mr. Q said, "Okay, everything is running smooth again. I can step outside."

He now left the restroom laughing, loudly.

"Mr. Cool, I know that you are going to give me your hot sex, play-by-play confessions at this party," I said, laughing.

Mr. Cool responded, "Oh, yes, shit, man! I'll tell you about this hot gorgeous blonde, she was handcuffed to the sex leather sling, and both her pretty feet were tied upward with her shining red sparkling nails. Her stunning, sexy, outrageous-looking net stockings were torn in her horny, private, hot juicy areas. Her beautiful tits were all oiled up, and she had a sensational, delicious, fucking warm temperature to boot. She continued to scream, 'Guys, I want all your big cocks, now! I want to be fucked hard! My pussy motor is running on overdrive! Fuck me silly, and bang me fucking hard!'"

"Wow, a wild hot-as-hell confession."

He said, laughing, "I kept taking turns in her hot, sweet pussy, it tasted so fucking amazing with her pussy juice flowing, and it was so damn wet! At the same time, she was sucking my buddy's cock, and she was stroking another huge-as-hell cock. Two other gorgeous guys with big-ass fucking muscles were both tonguing her big-ass nipples. It was a hot fucking sight to see, my man!"

"Whoa." Mr. Cool the Winner said, chuckling, "After so much fun fucking, she finally wanted to be untied and unhandcuffed and released from the leather sling. Then her choice was to lie on her stomach in a stunning heart-shaped, bright-red bed that was stationed nearby for some hot-ass-fuck, wild sex. Well, we all took our horny fucking turns, and she took all of our horny cocks with a happy smile."

"Wow, amazing!"

She then screamed with excitement, "Release all your hot loads in my tight ass! I want to feel each load inside of me. I want it now! Now! Fucking now! Now! Give it to me now, you stud motherfuckers!"

"No wonder, my friend, you've got the biggest fucking smile!" I said with a big chuckle.

He responded, "Yeah, my man, my smile says it all. She took every last drop in her ass from us, and now I feel like a million-dollar motherfucker! This is a fucking morning to remember!"

"You're always so amazing, my friend."

"It's the only way to be, my cool Latino friend, my neat-ass favorite restroom concierge!" he responded with a big-ass grin.

"Talk later, my amazing cool dude."

Mr. Cool the Winner said with a big ass smile, "It's a big fucking boom! And, my man, its going to be another amazing day in fucking paradise! Love every moment!"

"Cool vibes. Cheers!"

"Cheers!"

What a hot, fucking party, and more upcoming, naughty, wild sex confessions to read with many laughs.

## Chapter Four
## A WILD, CRAZY STORY!

****

### An Early Sexual Morning on the East Coast

When there is a party at a tremendous, beautiful crib with all the amazing delights, there are always wild, crazy stories. The women coming in at the front door were just incredible, with their beautiful bodies, outstanding tits, amazing sexy dresses, incredible hair, and beautifully designed to perfection, and they smelled so awesome with their delicious scents. Oh, my, the incredible scenes to remember for a lifetime. No wonder these guys were so fucking aroused and ready for their horny cocks to explode!

I just flow with every situation and have one hell of a fun time. Let's get to the damn point! Everyone was at this party to have a fucking blast and to eventually get laid and feel so damn amazing again. That is the point of excitement. Guys continued to come in and out of the restroom and always had many interesting funny-ass confessions for yours truly.

### 1:30 a.m.

JJ, Mr. Lick Man said, "Dan the Man, it's another shit show beginning on the second floor!"

I responded, "JJ, Mr. Lick Man, enjoy the party. We will definitely talk later."

"Cool, my restroom dude of greatness. Later."

Another guy came in to take a piss. He said, "I just had a fine bitch suck my cock and drain my hot load in one of the amazing bedrooms.

This crib is fucking something else! It's a fantasy atmosphere, a fuck-fantasy place with all the delicious delights! And, now I need to piss so damn badly!"

I responded, "Yeah, I've heard from many who have arrived. It's been a dream for many of the guests who are from other countries. It was extremely nice that the host gave me a tour of this outstanding crib. It just leaves you speechless and breathless."

He then said, "Oh, fuck! This piss was the best yet. Hell, yeah!"

I said, grinning, "I am so damn glad you're feeling much better now."

"Here is your tip for being so understanding, my man!" he said, exuberantly.

I gave him a big grin and responded by saying, "Thank you so much for your generous tip. I'm sure you will have another confession to tell."

He said, chuckling, "I have another two beauties with huge tits ready to go, and they are very interested in a hot threesome with some hot, wild-ass sex!"

I asked, laughing, "Well, what the hell are you waiting for?"

"They went to the bathroom to powder their makeover."

### 1:40 a.m.

Another guy was standing at the urinal taking a piss. He heard our conversation and said, "They are doing more than that. I am sure they are licking their hot, wet pussies for a quick thrill. It's really more power to you that they are ready for some steamy, kinky, fucking hot, raw-as-fuck, amazing power drive, explosive sex!"

The guy who was waiting for the two beauties responded, "Hell, yeah! I am ready for my motherfucking power driver to burst with several loads!"

"That is a great start. It sounds so incredible! My gosh—two hot chicks with huge tits. Wow, definitely a tit man."

### 1:45 a.m.

His phone rang. The phone conversation was wild-as-fuck, and I could hear every word clearly on his loud speakerphone.

"Yes, I am ready to go party with you both," he said with a big ass grin.

Then he said, chuckling, "Do you like to wear a strap-on? I watch this on porn movies all the time—a chick is fucking another chick after they have enjoyed eating each others pussy."

She said, chuckling, "Yes, that's a turn on, but I was thinking about fucking your tight ass. Then, when you're ready to cum, I will switch positions, and I will take your hot loads in my hot, tasty mouth and swallow every drop down my passionate throat!"

He said, "I don't know about getting fucked in my ass—it sounds too kinky-as-fuck!"

She responded, laughing, "You never know until you try it."

He said, "I just don't know, baby doll." She said, "My strap-on-cock is nine inches and thick. I will start slow, and slowly get my play cock in your tight asshole with, of course, plenty of hot lube to loosen you up."

He said, proudly, "Allow me to fuck your hot pussy with my ten-inch black motherfucking glory cock! It will make me more at ease, and you will feel so fucking happy with a big sensational smile on your beautiful face."

She responded, laughing, "What the fuck! Okay, but then I will lube your tight asshole and fuck you silly as hell!"

He said, laughing, "I'm lubing your ass, baby!"

She then said, "I'll meet you outside the bathroom door. Your conversation has turned me on so fucking much that my delicious girlfriend is also ready. She is kinky-as-fuck, loves giving head, loves to be pounded in her beautiful ass, and loves to eat my sweet pussy with that great tongue of hers. We are ready for a hot fucking threesome, and anything goes, my Kinky Man!"

He said, "I can't wait, my hot, kinky-ass, bitch!"

She said, "Bye, my hot black stud, horny fucker!"

"Bye. See you in a few."

This was going to be a hot, kinky-as-hell threesome of hot pussy juices flowing and a hard cock with exploding loads. I love all my conversations with everyone of my fun clients. How can you not enjoy these off-the-wall outrageous sex talks?

## 1:55 a.m.

There was a knock at the bathroom door. I immediately opened the door and said, "Yes, may I help you ladies?"

"We are here for Kinky Man."

I said, "Yes, he is right here."

Kinky Man, just a few moments before, had the wild and outrageous speakerphone conversation. He approached the door and said, "Ladies, great to see you again! Please, let's go to bedroom ten. I've finally made the final arrangements with the host of this party."

The beauties, responded, "Let's sixty-nine! We are fucking horny as hell, and we need to give your black stallion lots of love!"

Kinky Man said, "Ladies, sounds so fucking amazing, but let's also try seventy-one—I will excite you both with my kinky-ass version, a totally different, sexy, thrilling spin."

Both ladies surprised, and asked, "Seventy-one? What the fuck is that?"

Kinky Man answered, laughing, "I am going to tongue both of your hot pussies really sweet, and at the same time, I am going to finger-fuck you both with my two fingers up your beautiful asses. You will enjoy every fucking minute of my seventy-one." He was so damn ready for a hot-as-fuck threesome.

Then, all three continued with their sexy and loose naughty conversation. They finally left the front door of the men's bathroom to explore their many sexual fantasies in a magnificent, ready-made, romantic bedroom setting to fulfill their wildest sex dreams with one hell of a fucking blast.

Both beauties were dressed-to-kill, big-breasted women with tight asses, nipples showing through their slutty, tight blouses. They wore sexy pumps, and they smelled so fucking amazing with their high-end perfumes. They were both ready for a hot, kinky sex in a sensual setting. This was going to be a night to never forget.

It's never a dull moment in the men's room, and why should it be? People drinking, having a great time, amazing conversations, and their horny drives come right out into a fantasy adventure of fun and pleasure. Oh, my, it's time to party and let loose and forget all your personal fucking-ass frustrations.

## Chapter Five
# AN UNBELIEVABLE STORY!

****

### A Brutal Hot Morning in Tampa Bay

Who could forget an unbelievable story? Of course, there is never a dull fucking moment at these parties. Hell, no! There's always a shit story to tell. This means another chapter to type. Stay tuned for another reality. You just never know what's around the corner.

### 1:00 a.m.

We greeted each other with a winning smile. A guy dressed in a stunning Hawaiian shirt, torn blue jeans, and sandals came in and said, "I've got to run to the stall!"

"Okay," I said. "There you go. I will close the door for you."

Another customer dressed in a sport coat, dress shorts, and comfortable slip-on shoes came in and said, "I've got to take a piss really bad!"

"How's your night been so far?" I asked, enthusiastically.

He answered, "It's been fucking grooving and lit as hell on motherfucking bells!"

"Wow, there you go. And, that's the way it should be all the damn time!" I said with my biggest winning smile and energized voice.

The first customer who had been in the stall taking a shit came out to the sink area. I quickly sprayed the air freshener. I stood their, stunned. I could not believe what I witnessed with my own eyes. The guy had shit all over both of his hands. "Here, you definitely need foaming soap. I see you have shit on both your hands. Wow!"

He said in a nervous tone, "No, I have to run to my wife. She is waiting for me outside this restroom."

I responded, "But, you have shit on both your hands, man, and it smells so damn bad! Please allow me to put foaming soap on your hands."

He ran out of the restroom so incredibly fast that the next customer in line said, "What the fuck? Mr. Shit Hands Man! You have shit on both your motherfucking hands, you nasty-ass fucker!"

In a cool, soft voice, I replied, "I can't believe what I just saw. There are two rolls of toilet paper in the stall that he could have used. Why would anyone wipe his ass with his own hands?"

From a short distance, outside the restroom, Mr. Shit Hands Man could be seen hugging his wife, who was wearing a beautiful, colorful blouse. He got shit all over her expensive-looking outfit.

Oh, my! What the hell just happened? Mr. Shit Hands Man didn't wash his hands, and now there was nasty shit all over his wife's beautiful blouse. You can't make this shit up.

### 1:15 a.m.

She then said, loudly, "You nasty motherfucker! You got shit all over my expensive blouse! I just bought this for our romantic weekend, you bastard! You fucking son-of-a-bitch!"

"Honey, please, I can explain. Please, honey!" he said, beginning to tear up.

Everyone in line, including yours truly, watched and listened to this very loud and very clear conversation. It was one of those "What the fuck? I can't believe it!" moments.

She removed her blouse and angrily rubbed his nasty shit all over his face. She was fuming and angrily said, "You ruined our romantic night, you fucking dick!" The wife continued to yell at him as she ran out of the club, sobbing into her hands.

That sure as hell didn't end well. All he needed to do was to take a minute of his time to wash his hands with foaming soap and dry them with a nice soft-hand towel—or even just use fucking toilet paper, then apply hand sanitizer. This guy was a barbarian.

**1:20 a.m.**

She was found many blocks away from the club, still crying deeply. He sat there, embarrassed, with his head down resting on his shitty hands.

A guy in line sarcastically said, "Mr. Shit Hands Man, you fucking blew it for not washing your nasty, shitty, motherfucking hands with all your fucking shit on them! No pussy for you tonight! Matter of fact, you will be jacking-off alone!"

Mr. Shit Hands Man looked directly at him, rolled his eyes, and said, "Yeah, I did, and I'm now in the fucking doghouse, a man's nightmare of pure fucking living hell!"

The customer said, "Mr. Shit Hands Man, the doghouse may be your last resort. She may be getting another guy who shows consideration toward a beautiful lady."

Mr. Shit Hands Man, said, "Well, you don't have to rub it in. Fuck me!"

The customer, responded, "Yeah, fuck you! What the fuck, Mr. Shit Hands Man? You still got shit all over your fucking hands, and now it's smeared all over your motherfucking face! You need to clean up before you get rotten tomatoes thrown at you!"

**1:35 a.m.**

Dejected, Mr. Shit Hands Man decided to leave the club with his head down, completely embarrassed.

Some other partygoer yelled at him, "You're a disgusting, fucker!"

This was not a good ending at all, yet it's another story of reality and sadness. Who knows what'll end up happening to them, but whatever it is, it will happen behind closed doors.

For everyone else, take time to wash your hands. You'd be surprised how often I need to remind grown people to wash their hands. I mean, just look at this situation with Mr. Shit Hands Man. What the fuck, you know? We all might have been in the doghouse sometime in our marriages, but to be locked in the doghouse with shit on both of your hands and shit smeared all over your face, it's just fucking unbelievable!

# Chapter Six

# SINGING HIS JINGLE!

****

### An Exuberant Morning at a Famous Beach

On a brutally hot night in Daytona Beach, inside this gigantic mansion, it was a cool seventy-two degrees, extremely comfortable. Everyone was dressed spectacularly, modeling their new outfits with an exquisite style and a kick of the neatest up-to-date fashions. There were so many amazing presentations.

The nice thing about this gig was that I got to meet people from all over the world. I find that so fascinating. Oh, yeah, an amazing night would surge with another big blast. Of course, the night continued with exuberance. I really enjoy the many accents from all over the world, and the great conversations continue to sizzle with amazing excitement. The early morning hours arrived, and more food and drinks were served as the celebration continued with so much damn fun.

### 2:05 a.m.

He called himself, Mr. D the Smooth Man from the Bahamas. He was a distinguished, talented young man dressed in a sharp, stunning grey suit with a colorful bow tie that stood out with many bright colors. He had tons of money coming out of his pockets, and no doubt, he had the biggest and loudest naughty potty mouth that could sure as hell be heard from a good distance. He had no fear. He just did it his amazing way. And, no one would be able to stop his total exuberance.

He finished using the stall and then was ready for foaming soap and a nice, soft-hand towel.

We talked some. He said, "Mr. Dan the Man, your fucking service is cool, smooth, my man. I am going to sing my original horny-ass motherfucking song to everyone in this bathroom."

I said with my exuberance, "Mr. D, sing it, man. The bathroom stage floor is all yours!"

**2:15 a.m.**

Mr. D sang with his beautiful, powerful, and his smooth-as-hell baritone voice.

> Oh, yes, I am so fucking happy!
>
> I am here tonight to get my horse sucked.
>
> Oh, my, those beautiful, delicious women
> get my big horse rocking on.
>
> She puts those big tits all over my face, and my
> tongue licks those big, hard nipples.
>
> Now, I slide my big horse between those beauties until I
> shoot my big fucking load all over her amazing body.
>
> Now, I feel like a million bucks, Yes, I am relieved.
> My big horse feels so fucking great!
>
> I have the biggest smile now, oh, yes. I am so
> fucking happy. Yes, baby, baby, baby.
>
> I love you so much as you rock my big
> horse with the greatest pleasure.
>
> Now, I am ready to lick my sweet pussy, oh, yes, baby, baby, baby.

I am getting roused again. I am so fucking happy. Now, I am ready to slide my big horse in your wet, juicy pussy!

Oh, baby, baby, baby. Oh, yes, your pussy is so tasty, sweet, and we fit so fucking amazingly together, yes, baby.

I love you so much. Love your beauty on that magnificent bed, and lick you from head to your lovely toes, baby, baby, baby.

Let me slide my big horse and romance you all fucking night long.

I'm so fucking happy, baby! Let's do it again in our romantic setting.

All fourteen of the men who were present in the men's restroom gave a rousing, standing ovation! Many talented people attend these big-time mansion parties. You never know who you will meet having a lot of fun, enjoying every sensational moment.

**2:30 a.m.**

"Wow!" The many background voices all around the bathroom echoed.
Mr. D said, "Thank you!"
"You can really sing and entertain, Mr. D! Wow, man. Wow!" The host said in an excitable laughter.
"Keep cheering! Wow!"
Mr. D, responded, "Oh … my … gosh!"
"Let's get fired up! It's still early at this party!" said a big-time businessman after finishing pissing in the urinal.
"This is lit in this winning fucking moment!" A famous rapper said with exuberance.
"You need to be on Broadway," said a famous actor. "Mr. D, the stage is so motivating with bright lights, and it is so fucking lit with paradise all around you, my man!"
Mr. D said, "Wow!"

"Here is my business card, Mr. D. Call me Friday afternoon!" A talent agent responded with an exuberant, winning smile.

Mr. D said, "I will. Thank you! My gosh!"

What a night, and we still had a long way to go. This party was off-the-fucking chain, and the biggest blast was still to come! Wow!

"It's time for another cocktail. Your best Scotch on the rocks, please. Oh, thank you so much, and here's your generous tip. You deserve it! Well, I see a gorgeous stripper just walked in," said a big-time movie producer at the bar outside the men's restroom.

Hell, its always time for another confession for my future manuscript.

## Chapter Seven
# DON'T FUCKING FREAK OUT!

****

### A Night to Remember in Orlando

The setting was spectacular—a cool morning in one of the biggest mansions I've ever seen. Wow! It was a celebration party for creative artists from all over the world. They came in the wildest, craziest-ass, freaky costumes and were ready to party hard and get fucked-up, feeling so damn amazing.

And, the conversations were madly wild and entirely off-the-fucking wall.

A few guys came into the luxury men's bathroom all at once. I introduced myself to the ten guys who were present, dressed in their wildest costumes.

### 8:15 p.m.

"Hi, I am Dan the Man. I will be your concierge for the entire night, for this grand celebration party. I will be stationed here in the Men's Spectacular Elite Bathroom!" I said with my exuberant smile.

A customer immediately yelled from one of the stalls, "I am here for the hot pussy, whipped cream, and strawberries!"

I said with excitement, "You should have a grand selection of beauties here tonight! No problem whatsoever!"

He said, "A wild orgy would be an amazing party tonight!"

"You never know what's going to happen at any of these big parties!" I chuckled.

He left the stall, washed his hands, and gave me a generous tip.

"Thank you so much."

"Always my pleasure. Well, its time to cruise around and check out the new arrivals. I'll catch you later," he said, chuckling.

Another customer walked in. Mr. Freak introduced himself. I responded by saying, "My pleasure, Mr. Freak, I am Dan the Man." Cool! Mr. Freak asked with a big grin, "Are there any freaky chicks here at this party?"

I answered with my distinctive laugh, "I wouldn't know." Then I asked, "When you say freaky chicks, what are your specifics?"

"My freaky chicks must enjoy eating pussy and getting fucked in their tight asses at the same time," Mr. Freak answered with a big grin.

"Okay, interesting. I've seen some wild-ass parties in the past, so you never know when a hot freak is going to arrive," I said, chuckling.

He said, "Really, a hot-ass-freaky chick would do anything and be up with you all fucking night long—any sexual fucking fantasies you desire!"

"This would be a great time to check if your freak has arrived at the front door," I said, grinning.

Mr. Freak said, "Yeah, let me leave and scope the view for my freaky-ass chicks. I am horny as hell, man, and I am ready to explode my hot, milky, motherfucking tasty load!"

"Okay."

I love being involved in these's conversations. I always have so much damn fun with all of them, and it's no big deal. In my view, it's just another typical night at my office. Two hours passed, and the restroom continued to be an extremely busy place with hundreds of wild-ass fucking confessions.

**10:15 p.m.**

Mr. Freak once again entered the restroom and said, "My Man, I met a couple of hot freaks, and they both delivered big time!"

I said, "That's great Mr. Freak! I am sure that you are entirely satisfied with their hot presentation."

"It was a fucking dream come true—so damn amazing!" Mr. Freak responded with a big-ass smile.

"I am so happy for you!"

"The best, tastiest pussy in the world, and they were even giving me a fucking side show—their hot tongues were going really smooth, tonguing each other until their climax ventured to the top of the highest motherfucking mountain! It was so beautiful to see a live fucking sex show! Then they both took my hot motherfucking load and swallowed it while I gave them my biggest fucking smile!" Mr. Freak said, laughing and smiling with his sparkling gold grills that stood out.

"Wow! This must have been some sight to never forget, Mr. Freak!"

He responded, "Yeah. Their tongues were beautifully arranged to perfection. In other words, my man, they both perfectly executed like no other, and then it turned out to be my motherfucking cock, a bulging rouser, that I finally exploded with my big-ass smile!"

"That was a beautiful, quick lovemaking session. They showed their true fantasies and explored their hot sexual pleasures with total satisfaction."

He responded, "Oh, yeah, my man. Your talks are so fucking for real. It's so damn great being loved."

"Mr. Freak, my pleasure. It's always real with all your smooth talks. I love them all!"

He said, laughing, "I always appreciate you, my passionate man of the motherfucking hour!"

"And, I always appreciate you."

"Oh, yeah, my man, you're cool as fuck!" Mr. Freak responded, smiling again with his sparkling gold grills.

"Okay, my friend," I said with my winning smile.

"Bye, my fucking friend, the best restroom concierge in the whole entire world!" he said, chuckling.

*"Adios, mi amigo,"* I said, chuckling, as well.

*"Sí, amigo—que bueno,"* Mr. Freak said with his exuberant, winning laugh.

Yes, let's keep it going with many more naughty confessions. It's lit with another fucking blast.

# Chapter Eight
# WHAT THE FUCK ... IS THAT?

****

**An Unusual, Unexpected Early Morning in Jacksonville Beach**

It was a Friday morning to remember. You never know who will arrive in the men's restroom as the party is winding down. Only a few survivors were left at what had turned out to be the biggest sex party of the year. Wow!

I had seen nothing but big, lit smiles. Some were completely drained and had nothing left. Their dry milk cartons could not produce any more loads. They'd exploded all their hot loads and had nothing left to offer.

**3:34 a.m.**

As one customer finished at the urinal, he said, "You can shoot your motherfucking load only so many fucking times, and then it's time to go night-night."

"None of us has the power of the universe, you know," said another customer.

The bathroom door opened. Mr. B, a middle age man who was a regular at these parties was just banged up and hardly able to walk. The dress he wore was torn in several places, was wearing seven-inch pumps with the wildest-looking net stockings that were ripped to shreds.

A guy at the urinal turned around and asked, "What the fuck … is that?"

Another customer opened the stall door and said, "That's Mr. B. He is a cross-dresser who goes by the name, Miss Bango. He got teamed up with two guys and three gals at this party. It was wild and so damn crazy—the wild-ass leather sling fest as he wanted to get banged so badly."

Miss Bango is now walking slowly towards the stall.

Miss Bango, loudly said, "I have to go to this stall. I am in so much damn pain!"

I responded by saying, "Miss Bango, take your time. I will be leaving here in about forty minutes."

"Well, what the fuck! I might take the full forty minutes to regroup from my sore cock and my very sore asshole!" Miss Bango said with a painful look.

"As always, I will be the last one to leave, so take your time."

### 3:52 a.m.

There were very strange noises coming from the stall.

With a concerned high-pitched tone in my voice, I asked, "Miss Bango, are you okay?"

Miss Bango said in a high-pitched voice, "I am struggling. I just removed two feet … of quarter size marbles … out of my asshole! Oh, I am so much damn pain!"

"What?"

After I handed a customer a hand towel at the sink, a customer answered, "Well, we did not need to know about your strange-ass, fucking, freaky-ass-shit fantasies!"

"Wow!"

Miss Bango asked, "Is there a medic at this party? My ass is bleeding so badly!"

"Sorry to hear that, Miss Bango. Yes, there is a medic. I will call them immediately on my walkie."

I called the security team, "Security, security, please inform the medic team that we need medical assistance in 'Men's Room Star' immediately. Thank you."

"Copy that, Dan."

A wild-looking man entered the restroom and said, "Miss Bango really enjoyed the sex leather sling. He was tied with chains, doing some heavy poppers and continuous shots of whiskey. It really got out of reach and so fucked-up—he wanted a group power drive, wild, ass-fucking, kinky-ass sex!"

"Really?"

The medic team showed up in a matter of thirty-seconds to assist Miss Bango with her bleeding issues. The medic said, "Wow, Miss Bango needs some medical attention immediately. The hospital will definitely assist further."

The nearby hospital was about ten minutes away.

Another guest walked in the restroom and said, "What the hell happened to Miss Bango?"

At the same time, the last stall user flushed, came out, and said, "He was gang fucked, banged, silly as hell!"

The guest said, "What the hell!"

Miss Bango was now ready to go to the hospital with the assistance of the paramedic team. Once he was in the ambulance, the sirens sounded loudly on the grounds of the enormous mansion.

Miss Bango finally said to the paramedic team, "I had way too much fun, and definitely had extremely too much anal sex, but I loved every minute of it!"

### 4:25 a.m.

"Wow, this has been some unbelievable reality scene."

Now, I said to the remaining three guys left in the bathroom, "Let's hope all goes well with Miss Bango, our prayers. It's now four twenty-five in the morning, guys, an unusual morning to never forget. See you next time."

"See you, my incredible Dan the Man!" said the remaining three.

"Happy Blessed Friday. I've got to get some sleep here at this mansion's guest quarters and head back to Tampa Bay for tonight's gig."

"Bye and drive safe."

"Thank you. Bye," I said, packing my presentation into my suitcase.

Having an open mind in this business is a big advantage. Keep reading, my readers. You don't want miss any upcoming chapters about the naughty and hilarious reality confessions.

## Chapter Nine
# THE PITCHER BEER MAN!

****

### An Unusual Private Party to Never Forget

Private parties can be fun, interesting, outrageous, humorous, and kinky. These wild parties sometimes turn into nude parties. And, then there is always the unexpected. It was a hot-as-hell day outside, and a nice cool temperature inside. The guests came in dressed in casual clothes with flip-flops or sandals. It was perfect for a dress-down night and to have so much damn fun—and of course, to be naughty for another night.

### 7:10 p.m.

My first guest was a very interesting character. The Pitcher Beer Man introduced himself as an exuberant, young man, dressed all in grey with a bright orange baseball cap, and he had a cold pitcher of beer with him.

He said, "Dan the Man, this is a great night to get fucked-up on cold pitchers of beer!"

I responded by saying, "Hey, as long as you're having fun!" I then asked, "I'm sure you have a driver at the end of this party?"

"Hell, yes, I do!" he answered, taking a big gulp from his cold, frosty pitcher.

I said with a big grin, "Great, man. Enjoy every minute of this hot party."

"The night will get wilder as it continues," he said with a deadpan look.

I responded, "Oh, yeah, it always does. This sexy host always throws big parties."

"Her giant tits belong all over my face!" he said, chuckling.

"Wow, she is definitely the main attraction."

The Pitcher Beer Man took more big gulps of beer and said, "I need another pitcher."

I said with a big grin, "The host has ten cold kegs of beer, so help yourself, and check out the delicious gourmet foods."

**7:20 p.m.**

He left the men's bathroom.

Two minutes later ...

I said, smiling, "Great to see you again."

"I got to take another piss!" he said, frowning. "I didn't bring my wife to the party this time around." He continued to piss and took another two gulps of his cold beer.

I responded, "Everything okay?"

The Pitcher Beer Man said, "She needed some me time. We have an open marriage relationship. She is having two big studs from the Bahamas over to our pad for a hot fucking threesome."

"Oh, okay," I said in a low-key voice.

He said with a grin, "Don't be surprised. Whatever she wants, it's all right with me. It spices things up with a big motherfucking twist!"

"It's definitely spicy, hot, and never dull. Doesn't this bother you at all?"

The Pitcher Beer Man answered, grinning, "Hell, no! It's our mutual agreement and understanding. We love having an open marriage."

"Really, I must say, this is a very interesting confession. Wow."

He responded, saying, "Yeah, she likes big black cocks in her hot, tight asshole. She likes the other one to pound her delicious pussy. If a third shows up, she loves sucking his cock until she drains him completely dry."

"Wow, I didn't need to know all that. This is really a wild confession."

The Pitcher Beer Man said, laughing, "You see it in porn movies all the fucking time!"

"Okay."

He responded, "I just can't satisfy my wife. I just don't have a gigantic monster BBC, but I do have a wicked, good-sized tongue for her hot pussy, and I love to lick her lovely, tasty asshole. Then, I fuck that tight asshole!"

"Okay, so when you go home—"

He said, chuckling, "We still sleep in the same bed, and we never mention our fantasies that we have achieved. This keeps our relationship discreet and healthy, and, to us, it's our normal fucking life."

"I've got to have your confession in my book—do you mind? I am a writer," I said with my pleasant voice.

"No, not at all. It should delight other couples and encourage them to have open relationships. They can survive with the gusto of happiness," he said, smiling.

We exchanged business cards so we could contact each other.

### 7:35 p.m.

"I will draft up a release form. I will type the entire dialogue. This way you will be able to look it over, make all the necessary changes, accept it, and then sign the agreement so I can have this story for my future manuscript."

The Pitcher Beer Man said with a grin, "Oh, hell yeah, Dan the Man! I have so many stories to tell you. My wife likes me to use a big black dildo on her girlfriend. It reminds her of those exuberant, black huge cocks. And, when her girlfriends come over, it gets them feeling so fucking amazing!"

"Oh … my … gosh! I will save that material for another book. I have an overflow of hundreds of real stories."

He said, laughing, "No fucking problem, my man. I need to check out this hot, sexy party."

"It really does get wild and crazy, man!"

"Thank you, Dan the Man."

"No problem. Enjoy this crazy, wild-ass party with a hot blast," I said, chuckling.

"Bye. Be cool," he said with a grin.

"Bye. Have an incredible time."

## DAN THE MAN

Wow, having a blast with all of these wild-ass conversations. I keep it going having great fun. It always feels and sounds so damn amazing.

## Chapter Ten
# WHAT THE HELL IS GOING ON?

****

### A Clearwater Beach Private Party

It was a beautiful Sunday night. The amazing private party overlooked the beach. The waves were so magnificent, and the beach was so peaceful. The ribs were cooking on the huge outdoor grill along with the steaks. The smell of the great sauces together made all the many guests hungry to chow down.

**10:10 p.m.**

Two wild young ladies were hanging outside the men's restroom and flirting with the guys who were approaching the restroom. This was a huge mansion with many delights and so many attractions.

"This is going to be the biggest party of the year!" The host announced on his mansion's loud-ass speakers.

"What the hell is going on?" A male guest questioned the two young ladies, who were arguing about who had the biggest size tits.

One of the ladies responded to the male guest, "Fuck-off, you cockbite!"

Security came over and calmed the two young ladies. It did take a few minutes, but they both apologized to the male guest, as well as to security.

**10:25 p.m.**

The two young ladies were finally calm, laughing, and having a fun conversation. DJ XO finished pissing at the urinal and said, "I have a tape measure. I will measure both their tits and announce the winner during my signing of the greatest hits show."

"That will hopefully stop any future catfights and boob arguments."

"Yeah, Dan the Man. I tell you, both these chicks are incredible fucking knockouts with great, huge, shining motherfucking headlights!" said DJ XO, chuckling.

I responded, "I enjoy both of them with their enormous headlights. How can anyone not enjoy these hot-as-hell beautiful sights?"

DJ XO said, "Oh, hell, yeah, Dan the Man! I can't wait any longer! It's time to measure those big fucking tits!"

I said, laughing, "Enjoy every minute of the sizing, my friend."

"I plan to very closely. This will be a special treat of the night," DJ XO responded with his expression, a big happy smile.

"You got it made, DJ XO."

I opened the bathroom door quietly to check out the measurement session, and everything was going as planned. The two young ladies were calm, cool, laughing, and enjoying the friendly competition.

**10:35 p.m.**

DJ XO, said, "Ladies, it's a tie. You're both size forty. Wow, you both win the grand prize—a getaway weekend at my beach pad with yours truly."

The first young lady, responded, "Hell, yes!"

The second young lady, responded, "With your huge big shaft, we will have the hottest threesome and any fucking thing you want, you good-looking hot stud-man!"

"Okay, ladies, I have to run and spin some more music. I am the main man tonight," said DJ XO. His exuberant voice was so damn incredible.

## 10:45 p.m.

DJ XO, took off to spin his music. The ladies, still outside the men's restroom door, kept their blouses off and started sucking on each other's nipples. What an amazing sight! There is nothing like a private party with a lot of unexpected attractions to definitely rouse everyone.

Another customer entered the restroom and asked, "What the hell is going on?"

I answered, "Just another amazing, fun party with all the delicious delights. Just stick around. This party is just starting to rock with the amazing fireworks right in front of you."

The customer said, "That's a big cock rouser!"

"It sure is. Have a spectacular party."

"Fuck, yeah!" The customer responded with exuberance.

Until next time and another story to tell, stay tuned for more delights. There is a never a dull fucking moment with vampire hours.

## Chapter Eleven
# HOT FOURSOME COMING UP!

****

### A Blast in Ft. Lauderdale Beach

It was another hot morning, but beautiful though—clear skies and beautiful people getting ready to take their hot spots, getting ready for another hot, sexy night at another mansion spectacular.

### 6:00 p.m.

It was a laid back moment. I decided to check things out away from the bathroom for a few minutes while snacking on a healthy protein bar.

I knew these two amazing customers who were my regulars. This very clear conversation took place outside the men's restroom area located near the mansion balcony.

Mr. M the Hip Man was so cool. He was a talker and so damn smooth. He said to Sunshine with a happy grin, "You have been my close buddy for nearly fifteen glorious years. It's another beauty, Sunshine."

Sunshine, with his striking smooth talk, said, "Yeah, Mr. M, it's so fucking cool, my fucking number-one bro!"

Mr. M responded, "Fucking, yeah! It would a great day for hot sex with those beauties near the water on this hot-as-hell beach."

Sunshine said with enthusiasm, "No doubt. The beach always makes me horny as hell!"

"Let's have a great time with those two fine bitches over there," said Mr. M the Hip Man.

They both wasted no time. They connected and then made quick plans with their new beautiful lovelies coming to a spectacular mansion beach night party.

### 8:35 p.m.

They arrived with their beach beauties, all tanned. They really stood out of the hundreds of people. They all came in with their positive vibes, and everyone noticed their favorable entrance.

A few minutes later...

Mr. M the Hip Man and Sunshine finally arrived in the bathroom. They were two exuberant, exciting men, both drinking straight shots of rum.

I said with a positive vibe, "Hello, guys, great to see you again."

"Hello, Dan the Man, my fucking man!"

"That's so cool, guys."

Mr. M the Hip Man said, "See you back in a few minutes, we have an important call coming in, need to take it."

"Look forward. See you both in a few."

Positive vibes were already flowing in the early night hours in the men's restroom. That's the only way it should be—no excuses whatsoever.

### 8:50 p.m.

Mr. M the Hip Man and Sunshine entered the restroom once again. Sunshine went directly to the sink area.

Sunshine said, "Oh, my man, soap and a hand towel, hell, yeah!"

"Here is a nice, soft-hand towel," I responded with my winning smile.

"Mr. M the Hip Man, always appreciates this amazing fucking service from Dan the Man. Wow!" said Sunshine in his vibrant baritone voice.

Mr. M the Hip Man said, "I see, Sunshine, my hot massage fucking dude."

Sunshine asked as he was chuckling, "Dan the Man, do you know if we have to put our dough up for a room to have a hot fucking foursome?"

"Yes, you do. Let me contact the host for you," I answered with a smile.

"We have two fine bitches that are bisexual, and they want to tongue their hot pussies. They both want to give the new daddies a fucking hell of a grand sex show and then make it a hot motherfucking foursome, even switching our dates during this steamy, hot-as-fuck sexual blast!" Mr. M the Hip Man was excited to say.

"Sounds so amazing," I said. "I will hand you my phone. The host, Ali-Mo is on the line."

"Thank you, my man," said Sunshine, who was now speaking to the host on my cell phone. "Thank you, and yes, Ali-Mo, sounds incredible!"

"It's a done deal, Mr. M the Hip Man. We have 'The Sexy' exclusive room. The room concierge will be waiting for us, and we will pay the dough with one motherfucking credit card," said Sunshine.

"Great news, guys. That's awesome!" I said, grinning.

"How are the rooms, my man?" Sunshine asked with a chuckle.

I answered, "The rooms are just incredible. A huge, round bed for your fantasy pleasures, a bar with a great selection of drinks, an extra-sized shower, and a beautiful Jacuzzi. You will have an amazing fucking time. Sunshine, with your magical massage hands, you should drive both beautiful ladies crazy, with a hot nude party starting in the hot Jacuzzi."

"Yeah, my man. It will be a hot motherfucking foursome!" said Mr. M the Hip Man, laughing with a positive vibe.

I said with a positive chuckle, "Enjoy the night to never forget. Boom and another fist boom! Blow it up!"

"Oh, fuck, yeah! Another fist boom, my fucking man! Blow it up!"

As they both were walking out, they quickly stopped and turned around, and Mr. M the Hip Man, asked, "My fucking man, do you have raincoats and some hot oil lotion in small bottles?"

"I do have both items for your hot beauties," I answered with a big grin.

Sunshine said, "We will take a half-a-dozen extra-size raincoats to protect our motherfucking huge black-beauty cocks and four bottles of your hottest sex lotions. Yeah, baby, nice and hot! We will entertain their fine tasty asses and those amazing fine tits to suck on, and it will be a great fucking explosion with our fucking hot juices, my man!"

I responded, "No problem, guys. Here you go."

Mr. M the Hip Man responded with a happy laugh, "Here is your big-ass motherfucking Benjamin tip, my man, for the greatest fucking service!"

**9:10 p.m.**

I responded with a big smile, "Wow, thank you so much for your generous tip, guys. Wow! The room concierge just texted me. He is waiting on your arrival and to personally hand you both your keys."

"Oh, fuck, yeah! Thank you, my fucking man. It's a big nude-ass fucking party, and this will be an amazing motherfucking time!"

"My pleasure, guys."

They both then responded with excitement, "Wow, time for another fist boom! Fuck, yeah! Boom, and blow it up! The motherfucking bitches are going to an amazing fucking! Yeah, we are going to get laid and be so fucking happy!"

"Okay, this is lit!"

About a minute later …

They both started singing, "All night long … all morning long … it's time for a hot, wild-ass motherfucking party!"

I always have a blast with all of these funny-ass confessions. It doesn't matter if the conversations have profanity and sexual remarks from each client. It makes them feel so damn amazing because, in my eyes, they are amazing clients.

# Chapter Twelve
# HOT, WILD, SEX TALK!

****

### A Hot-as-Hell Sex-Driven Night in South Florida

These hot nights are to cherish and remember. Beautiful people, hot young things, dressed to kill, smelling just sensational, and none of them mind showing their hot bodies. I mean, they are all gorgeous, with the hottest boobs and those hot, tight asses. No wonder these guys are walking all over this party with hard cocks in their tight-ass pants and their mouths drooling with saliva, their tongues hanging out like the tongues of young puppies. No doubt, everyone is in heat and on overdrive with their horny-ass images.

The neat thing about this restroom gig is that I meet people from all over the world. I have an open mind, I flow with each given conversation, and I never make a big deal about their sexual orientations. In my first book, *Hi, I Am Dan the Man, Your Concierge*, I wrote, "We are all human beings of equal standing. I believe in equality." There are no excuses whatsoever deviating from this powerful statement.

### 11:15 p.m.

A striking transgender woman dressed in a bright green outfit over her big forty-inch tits walked in the restroom and asked to use the urinal. Her nipples were hard, noticeable through her sheer blouse, and she was wearing sexy six-inch pumps.

I answered, "No problem. There are a number of them. Obviously, they are all in gold." I then asked her, "How has your night been so far?"

She was now taking a piss standing at the urinal as she answered, "I am fine, gorgeous. Thank you so much! The vibes tonight are very positive and kinky as hell, which I fucking love."

I responded, "Well, that's great. It should be an interesting night for everyone here at this party."

She then proceeded to say, "I am definitely going to fuck one of these beautiful people in their tight asshole tonight! Their delicious ass will be mine all fucking night long! I will have my lucky delight screaming with joy!"

I responded, laughing, "Enjoy your fun night at this exuberant, fun party."

She said, "I fucking will, with a huge cum blast! Bye."

"Bye."

**11:22 p.m.**

As she walked out of the men's restroom, another couple walked in holding hands. One was a tall, handsome Latino male dressed in a navy tux, a wild bow tie of many beautiful blended colors, shining blue shoes, and a standout positive image. His date was a transgender with a thirty-eight-inch bust, a tight ass, a sleazy bright red dress, sexy net slutty stockings, and an amazing beautiful smile.

They both approached the urinals side-by-side and started playing with each other's cocks and French kissing.

"You both! This isn't a cock stroke-off kissing bedroom! It's a restroom where you can piss and shit and proceed to your fun party! The host has respectable rules at these invitation-only sex parties!" I said in my firm tone.

"Okay, we were just in the mood for a damn stroke-off and a tongue quickie," The couple responded, grinning with their big white teeth. They finished their business of urinating, and I then provided them with foaming soap and towel service for their hands. The Trans said, "Thank you for this kick-ass fucking service! I do need some cigs."

I responded, "No problem. I have a great selection of them."

She said, "The pack of the natural cigs is fine. They burn longer than the regulars do."

"Great! I just opened a new pack of cigs, and I will light your first cig," I said, happily.

She said, "Thank you for your professionalism."

I responded, "My pleasure, and thank you so much for your generous tip. Wow!"

**11:30 p.m.**

She told her date, "Before we leave this restroom, I need to lube my tight, horny, hot ass. I will just take one of the open stalls for just a few minutes. Don't leave me, my naughty cock-fucker!"

Her date said, "Okay, no problem. I want to see you get fucked really hard tonight in your hot, tight asshole, and get deep-throated with a gigantic, fucking thick cock—that's a fucking turn on for me, honey boo! Then, I can jack-off all over your beautiful face, and you can taste my hot leche load!"

After a few minutes, she finally left the stall with a happy-as-fuck smile.

She told her date, "Well, my ass is ready to be plowed and fucked hard. I want to scream tonight with happy tears!"

I said, "Wow! What a night ahead of you!" I then asked, "Do you need some condoms?"

She answered, "Sure, gorgeous, the big size. I want the biggest fucking cock at this party!"

"Here you go. Oh, my! Thank you for the generous tip!"

She responded with a big smile, "No fucking problem."

**11:38 p.m.**

I then said, "I know you both will have an exciting night."

She said, "We can't wait for some kinky, fucking hot, wild-ass fucking sex to take place! Our cocks are ready to go with a motherfucking blast, and our asses need lots of love!"

"Enjoy your sex blast," I said, laughing.

They left the restroom, and I still continued to laugh for a few minutes. I enjoy the hundreds of funny confessions each night.

# Chapter Thirteen
# SHIT, JIVE, AND EXUBERANCE!

****

### An Extremely Exuberant Night in Tampa Bay

It was an extremely hot Saturday night at one of the hottest nightclubs in the Bay area. So far, a nice crowd was enjoying their happy hour blast, and a lot of these same people were beginning to feel a bit overwhelmed. For a set price, you can drink all you want during the happiest four hours of your life. Yes, this was another night to remember. All of the friends, boyfriends, girlfriends, spouses, and secret sidekicks had come for a fun night out. And let's not forget all the amazing birthday parties that are enjoying their celebrations.

### 10:32 p.m.

It was time for another shit show once again in the men's restroom.

A customer walked into the men's restroom complaining of an upset stomach. He was well dressed in a bright green sports coat, a tan shirt, green dress shorts, and brown sandals. It was a striking outfit that stood out in the crowd. His veneer of discomfort told me his story right away. It was written all over his face. He said in agony, "I've had a tremendous amount of pain in my stomach for the past hour or so."

"I am Dan the Man. I will be your concierge until closing. I'm really sorry to hear that you're not feeling well."

He passed a hand over his sweaty forehead and muttered, "Wow, man, I haven't taken a good shit in about a week and a half. This is just bringing me down, and I can feel my stomach growling constantly. I believe that my shit might be coming really soon."

I responded, "Wow, that doesn't sound good. Hopefully you will feel much better. Why don't you check out the stall toilet? This might be your time to poop that out of your system."

He then said with a grumpy-ass frown, "I'm going to hit the fucking shitter and take the biggest dump of my life! Oh, shit, man, I can feel it coming!"

I said, grinning, "Have at it, man, the stall is all yours. I have plenty of air freshener, so do your thing, and I will continue to spray down the bathroom."

**10:37 p.m.**

He entered, and I heard an orchestra of farts trumpeting from the stall. It smelled like ass. It was so damn bad! He kept flushing and flushing. I sprayed the air freshener as my teary eyes began to cross.

His shit smelled so fucking horrible.

He said in a high-pitched voice from the stall, "Holy shit! I am shitting my brains out! I didn't think my shit was going to feel like a heavy stream of water coming out of my asshole!"

I responded in a high-pitched voice, "Just take your time! I am going to spray some more air freshener! It's really very strong in here! Wow!"

He yelled from the stall, "Yes! It stinks like sewer! It smells like a pile of rotting plague corpses! It sure doesn't smell like one of your expensive colognes!"

I laughed. "Hell, no! It sure as hell doesn't!"

There were a number of guys outside the restroom forming a line. One-by-one, they all filtered in to use the urinal, and some were waiting for the stall to be open. This really was a tiny-ass bathroom.

### 10:40 p.m.

A guy in line shrieked, "What the fuck! That guy is destroying the stall! Shit, man. Did something die in his stomach and then fucking rot in his goddamn asshole? He's so fucking disgusting!"

Another guy in line whispered, "He must have eaten a dead animal."

Then a third guy said, "Wow! That's like a week's worth of shit! He smells so fucking rotten!"

I kept spraying air freshener in the bathroom to alleviate some of the shit smell, but my watering eyes were telling a different story than my forced smile. I sure as hell didn't want to have to call 911 in case someone passed out from this guy's rotten bowels! I tried to lighten the mood with the air freshener. I said, "Now that smells a little better, right?"

I never want any of my customers to suffocate from someone else's horrible shit smell. I sprayed even more air freshener, a baby powder scent. I thought, Okay, now it really smells like baby powder. Baby powder is better than rotten shit, and that's a hell of an improvement.

### 10:45 p.m.

A fourth guy in line screamed, "Your fucking shit is fucking horrible!"

The customer inside the stall heard everything, and he didn't like it. He responded, "I heard that! I should come out and rub my nasty shit all over your motherfucking faces!"

A guy responded impatiently, "Oh, yeah? Well, when you come out of that fucking stall, I'm gonna piss on your fucking face, you fuckwad!" He was standing in line, waiting his turn, legs crossed, and leaning against the wall with one arm, looking down at the floor. He'd broken his seal a little while ago and was desperate to unload his bowels.

The guy who shit his brains, towered over the stall door once he stood, looked rough. He was built like a linebacker and was in excellent shape with a sleeve of colorful tattoos. He looked like a solid 265 pounds. The stall door just flew open.

This dude was fuming. He grabbed his crotch as he scanned the bathroom for the source of anger. "Where is that fuckwad that wants to piss on my face? I am ready for his motherfucking ass! He needs my fucking whip!"

The entire line of ten guys, none of whom were more than five and a half feet tall, ran quickly like cockroaches.

The big guy boomed with laughter, "What a bunch of pussies! They got some little baby balls! Fuck all of them!"

The air freshener finally alleviated the stinky shit smell in the entire restroom.

**10:55 p.m.**

"Here is some foaming soap for your hands."

The big guy accepted the soap and asked, "Well, do you have hand towels? I don't want those fucking paper towels! They're dog shit!"

"But of course I have hand towels. I never use paper towels. It's unprofessional."

"Great! By the way, you can call me Mr. Muscles, because I'm so goddamn big!"

"Sure, Mr. Muscles," I said, chuckling.

"All right, Dan the fucking Man. I like your shirt with your own logo. It looks fucking amazing!"

"Thank you, Mr. Muscles."

Smiling, he said, "You're welcome, dude."

I now applied foaming soap on the palm of Mr. Muscles's hand. I also provided him excellent towel service, professionalism, and a knock-out presentation.

**11:00 p.m.**

"This soft-hand towel is the bomb, man. Your fucking service is so damn amazing!" he said with a big, goofy grin.

I smiled back and said, "Thank you so much, Mr. Muscles. I do appreciate your positive feedback."

Mr. Muscles, looking over his shoulder toward the restroom door, said sternly, "I think that those cock motherfuckers left the club for good!"

I responded, "Wow, you sure cleared the entire line! They were running out of here like there was no fucking tomorrow! No wonder they left—they might have even shit in their pants!"

"Yeah, they can't handle my bulging muscles. Anyway, I am going to check the partygoer's of this fucking club. I love those positive vibes out there."

"Pleasure meeting you, Mr. Muscles, and enjoy your exuberant night."

He stopped, turned his head to look directly at me, and said, "I got to get a hot babe with some incredible tits. And, dude, you know, I gotta go for a nice, tight ass to go along with it. No doubt, my man, I need to release my overdue load soon!"

I responded, "I understand. Well, you have a tremendous selection here tonight. There are so many beauties. Do enjoy your conversations with all of them."

There are so many shit talks each night. It's just another typical crazy and lit night at a nightclub. There is never a dull moment, and why should there be? It's always exciting.

### 11:10 p.m.

Mr. Muscles was indulging in conversations at the huge patio bar. He came across some good friends and some new people who were cheerful, fun, and ready to party hard with him.

Mr. Muscles entered the restroom again and gave me an update. He said, "Dan the Man, I have just been invited to a wild orgy party at some mansion about ten minutes away, nearby. I am so fucking pumped! I gotta get back for the remaining details, man, and, wow! This piss really feels so fucking great! Oh, I'm so fucking relieved!"

I chuckled and said, "That's great, Mr. Muscles. I'm glad that all is going well, and that is really exciting news!"

The young, sexy lady who owned the huge mansion took command of the meeting at the bar area. She had a beautiful personality, a winning smile, and a great set of boobs. She invited sixty beautiful people to her party event.

### 11:15 p.m.

At her short meeting, she said, "I am going to have the best erotic fuck party at my mansion! I am so fucking excited to have you all!"

Mr. Muscles stated, "There is no damn reason why sixty horny, driven people like us can't all enjoy the thrill of an incredible fucking time at your party tonight and feel so fucking tremendous all morning long!"

"Oh, hell, yeah, Mr. Muscles, well said!" The voices sounded-off from the sixty invited guests.

"Lets all have another drink before we leave!" Mr. Muscles said with exuberance.

There is no doubt that everyone will have the biggest smile on their veneers, and why not? These invited men and women's objectives are to release their horny drives, and then they will have the exuberance to conquer the world and say, "What the fuck, I am ready to have an amazing night in paradise. It's so damn beautiful. Fuck, yeah!"

**11:30 p.m.**

"Now, lets all party, have fun, and really enjoy the mind-blowing sex!" Miss Z Sexy Babe, said enthusiastically.

Some excited customers hooted and hollered in response.

"Hell, yeah, Miss Z Sexy Babe, and thank you so much!"

"Let's get the fucking party started!"

Miss Z Sexy Babe responded, "Everyone, I will join in fully naked as well. I love both sexes."

"Let's get fucking bare-ass naked!" One guy shouted before chugging his cold beer.

They all left the club in a big party bus owned by Miss Z Sexy Babe. The partiers were ready to rock and roll. You could hear their exuberance from a great distance! It was an amazing sound of sixty happy, horny, high-profile people!

"It's party time folks! Hell, yeah, to nudity, sex, and amazing heavy metal music with the loudest beats!" Miss Z Sexy Babe said with her charm and high-spirited confidence. She then proclaimed loudly, "Hey, let's all get fucking naked and show our beautiful bods! It's now officially party time!"

It was one big fuck party for all of the hot invited partiers. It was time to get fucking naked, wild, and crazy. Some were even stripping down on the bus. The wild-ass party had just begun.

# Chapter Fouteen
# A SWINGERS SHOWCASE!

****

### A Hot Swingers Party in Daytona Beach

These beautiful people were arriving by the hundreds at this unbelievable mansion celebrity party. It was a breezy early morning with amazing outdoor weather of sixty-five degrees at the beach. This was going to be a fun, exuberant swingers party. The couples in attendance would be swapping their partners to the other's delight.

As the couples were walking into the main room, they were dressed in very little clothing. The beautiful young ladies were proudly showing-off their huge tits. They were dressed in skimpy shorts, and their sexy legs were just incredible. Most of the men were dressed in swim shorts and flip flops. They kept it simple and to the point because, in a short time, every couple would be nude and ready for some hot-as-hell, wild sex.

My men's bathroom for the night was all setup with my winning presentation. It was a huge men's room with all the amazing delights, including a spacious seating area where men could relax and watch whatever program they wanted, including hot porn movies with every flavor to choose from. This was an incredible setup for these invited men. There were even private rooms outside the bathroom for hot sex with the gorgeous ladies or the same-sex flavor, whatever the men's preference was to be for that morning.

### 12:10 a.m.

My first customer walked in with a towel wrapped around him and said, "Wow! It's time to take a big piss!"

I said, "You have so many urinals to choose from. I can see that this party is going very well for you."

"My name is Dick the Snake. You will see me a few more times," he said, grinning.

"Pleasure to meet you, Dick the Snake. My name is Dan the Man." Dick the Snake said, "Great to meet you. This hot sex party has been an amazing fucking night so far. My wife and I already are swinging, and we already had some hot sex in a hot, private setting."

"That's awesome!" I said with a happy grin.

He responded while puffing on his menthol cig, "It's just one big-ass, wild orgy. I feel that I will score another gorgeous young lady very soon! Sir, I have your generous tip for the entire morning in this sealed envelope."

I said, "Thank you so much! I appreciate you! There are two young ladies in private room number three making passionate love with all types of sex toys and plenty of hot sex lube. And, the sign outside the room does state they're open for more fun. It's a fun thought to really consider."

He responded, "Hmm ... I will have to check that out."

"Sure, why not."

Dick went to the private room located down the hallway from the men's bathroom. He went to check out the two gorgeous ladies.

### 12:25 a.m.

Mr. Malto the Magician walked in and said, "Dan the Man, what a fucking party! Everyone is swapping their spouses, getting their hot juicy, loads off, and pussy juice is just flowing all over the fucking place, man, all over this fucking mansion!"

"Sounds so damn amazing, Mr. Malto the Magician!"

"My man, do you have any raincoats? I need to protect my valuable power drill," he asked, discretely.

"Sure do. What size?" I answered in a whisper.

He responded with excitement, "Definitely the extra size!"

"Okay, no problem. How many do you need?"

Mr. Malto the Magician said with a happy grin, "Four. No problem getting four hot, sexy bitches at this party!"

"Thank you, for your generous tip."

He responded, "You're welcome, my fucking man."

At this time, there was a knock at the bathroom door. I went directly and opened the door.

## 12:35 a.m.

"Yes, may I help you, beautiful?" I said with a positive smile.

"My name is Honey Bunny. I understand that I can enjoy hot sex in the private room down the hallway from this bathroom. Is that correct? I am a sexy exhibitionist from L.A."

"Yes, you can, Honey Bunny. My name is Dan the Man. I will show you the way. Oh, by the way, Honey Bunny, this is Mr. Malto the Magician."

Mr. Malto the Magician said, "Pleasure to meet you, Honey Bunny. You look incredible, delicious, and sexy, baby!"

Honey Bunny responded, "Great to meet you, my handsome stud man. Come join me in the private room for some hot, tasty, amazing kinky sex!"

I said, "I will take you both to one of the spectacular private rooms, and then I will immediately come back to my bathroom duties. You both will have an amazing fun time!"

Both Honey Bunny and Mr. Malto the Magician entered the private room and immediately started French kissing, going at it with their loose tongues. It was a hot scene, with some hot-as-hell sex vibes.

Sex all over this place with naughty, exuberant vibes.

## Chapter Fifteen
# THE BEST PRANK EVER!

****

**A Beautiful Night with an Unexpected Twist!**

It was another beautiful night at an amazing nightlife spot in Tampa Bay, always a nice crowd with many great conversations. Happy hour had another thirty minutes left on the clock. The guys were coming into the restroom to take a quick leak and leave immediately to get their last happy hour drink before the deadline. Many things can happen with only a few minutes left.

**10:30 p.m.**

Mo the Slammer said exuberantly, "These happy hour drinks are fantastic—great bartenders!"

"Yes, Mo the Slammer, you have here many great bartenders," I responded.

"Yeah, getting a very good buzz with whiskey," he said with a slur.

"You only have a few minutes left!"

Mo the Slammer responded, "Yeah. I am going to drink one more and call for a ride back to my secret mistress who is kinky-as-fuck!"

I said, "Be cool, Mo the Slammer, and have a fun, sexy night."

Having a great sense of humor is a big plus. Enjoying the different topics can be a blast with so much damn fun.

## 10:40 p.m.

"Great to see you, PJ the Jock. Let's talk hockey."

PJ the Jock said, "Yeah, the hockey team is doing great!"

I responded, "Oh, hell, yes! Another great season! The Cup would be amazing, again!"

PJ the Jock said with a grin, "Hell, yes! They are kicking ass and scoring goals. Well, let me get back to my friend's birthday party. His date is a naughty stripper."

"Happy birthday to your friend, PJ the Jock," I said with a big smile.

"Thank you so much, my fucking bathroom guy who has so much amazing class!"

Jason Dillard now entered the restroom. We both gave each other a firm business handshake with a big smile. Jason is one of my regular customers, always with a positive mindset, a winning image, and the leadership qualities of success.

## 10:45 p.m.

I asked with a grin, "Jason, how have you been?"

Jason answered, "Great! I haven't been here in a while."

"How is work going?" I asked.

Jason answered, "I got a new job with the FBI."

I said, "Congratulations!"

Jason took out a business card and said, "This guy is wanted by the FBI and dangerous."

My eyes zeroed in directly to the business card, and I immediately had a really stunned look.

After a silent minute . . .

Jason and I busted out laughing so damn hard and continued to laugh for a few minutes. It was the funniest prank I've been involved with my many years in this business. This prank was so damn funny, and my stunned look said, "What the hell just happened?" Jason showed me my own business card with my headshot pic, setting it up as though I was the one who was wanted and dangerous. This was so damn hilarious! We both continued to laugh, hysterically.

To this date, we continue to laugh and laugh at the funniest prank Jason Dillard accomplished with his positive and settled laid-back approach: "The best prank ever on Dan the Man!"

I always look forward to all my conversations with Jason, and we will definitely continue to have many great laughs to come.

This wasn't a naughty story, but it was hilarious. Laughter is always so healthy with many good laughs.

# Chapter Sixteen

# BLOW-UP DOLLS AND SHEEP!

****

### A Delight of Wild Surprises in St. Petersburg

An amazing wild party was ready to start at a beautiful mansion near St. Petersburg Beach. The start time was 11 p.m., and the party was scheduled to end at around four or five in the morning. It was another night-to-early-morning gig working vampire hours again. The premier men's restroom, which had four urinals and four stalls, was in tip-top shape, decorated in so many outstanding colors.

### 10:40 p.m.

The host of this elaborate party approached me and said, "You're going to love my clients and my funny-ass pranks!"

I responded, "No problem whatsoever. I will have a fun time with the hundreds of laughs. It's always fun and exuberant."

The owner and host, Mr. Dom Freakinghowser, had blow-up sheep hanging from the ceiling, just above each urinal. And, he had creatively placed a blow-up doll in each of the shitters. Each upscale blow-up doll was decked out to perfection with a sexy-as-hell, very skimpy outfit and a beautiful wig, and each one of their mouths moved in a circular motion. On a set timer, every five minutes, each sexy doll would say a few words to rouse and excite each stall customer.

The brilliant host wanted to hear all about the different responses from each client. He thought that the responses would be off-the-wall and the funniest confessions of all time. He was absolutely correct! He also placed other prank sex toys throughout his mansion. It was a night to remember with all different types of sex pranks.

**11:10 p.m.**

These are the wild and off-the-wall responses from the men's restroom.

Customer number one, a man with a southern drawl, said, "Man, I am really taking a healthy piss. I am looking at that sheep hanging above my head. I tell you something—when I was a young fella, I grew up on a farm and fucked many sheep. I started very young fucking their pussies. Yeah, it was something else. My grandpa taught me to get those sheep and have some fun because it does feel like the real pussy."

I asked with a stern look, "Let me understand what you just said—you fucked sheep on the farm. Is this correct?"

The customer answered, "Sure did, many of them, all shapes and sizes. Man, I was a happy camper with always a smile. Well now, let me check out the fine-ass beauties here at this party."

I said with a surprise look, "I just don't know what to say. I guess . . . I'm in a state of shock. Do have a good time with the beauties here at this party."

He said, "Yes. I look forward to a great time!"

Customer number two said, in a high-pitched voice, from stall number one, "Gee, here I'm taking a shit, and I am actually getting roused up with this sexy blow-up doll! I mean, now I have a damn hard-on, and playing with my cock! Oh, fuck, now I'm stroking it!"

I said in a high-pitched voice, "We do not need to know your sexual details inside the stall!"

Just then, the blow-up doll in stall number one said, "Hey gorgeous, you want to play with me? My mouth is wet and ready."

Customer number two said in a high-pitched voice, "Holy shit! This sexy, slutty doll talks to you! What the fuck!"

I said, laughing, "Surprise! It's a shit show in the shit stall with a sleazy, slutty, horny blow-up doll! How do you like that?"

"Whoa!"

### 11:25 p.m.

Customer number three walked in and went directly to the urinal. As he was taking a piss, he said, "Yeah, that sheep hanging above my head ... oh, yeah! Used to grab their hooves, put their back legs in my cowboy boots, and ride that sheep silly as fuck! And then the sheep reacted with her unique sound—'Baaaaaaaaaaaaaaaaaaaaaaah, baaaaaaaaaaaaaaaaaaaaaaaaaah!' Man, what an awesome fucking! I fucked the hell of that sheep! I was a professional sheepfucker!"

I laughed and said, "Oh, really? Okay, another funny confession. There was another customer who was just here. He also had a sheep sex story to tell."

I continued to laugh, hysterically.

Customer number three responded, "Well, it was sheep then. Now its pussy time, and the host has many beauties. I just happen to be experienced with sheep fucking, but I am here at this party, naturally, for some hot, amazing pussy."

"Okay," I said, laughing.

Customer number four walked in and headed directly to stall number three. He opened the door and said, "Honey, allow me to join you. I've got to take a big-ass shit!"

The blow-up doll said, "Hey gorgeous, you want to play with me? My mouth is wet and ready."

Customer number four responded, "What the fuck! I did not expect this sexy doll to talk, and she is moving her hot mouth in a circular motion for my horny cock! Shit, man, oh, fuck!"

In a high-pitched voice, I asked, "How do you like the sexy doll now?"

"I am getting so fucking excited!"

I responded, "Just keep the door locked, but don't get excessively loud. I mean, you know, it's a men's restroom at a private mansion."

### 11:45 p.m.

Customer number two in stall number one was getting so damn excited, and his voice continued to get louder and louder. He said, "Yeah, bitch, suck my cock! Oh, yeah. I love your motherfucking mouth! Oh, yeah, here goes—I am going to shoot my fucking load! Yeah! That's the way! Oh, fuck, yeah, my kinky fucking bitch! Ah ... take it now! Fuck, yeah! Down your hot motherfucking throat! That's it! Take every drop of it! Ah ... Ah! Ah! Ah! Ah! Yeah ... Ah ... fuck ... yeah ... Ahhhhhhhhhhhhhhhhhh!"

I said in a high-pitched voice, "Well, we all heard you outside the stall! I'm sure now that everything is just so damn dandy! I am sure that you feel just on top of the fucking world!"

Customer number two responded in a low breathing voice, "Oh, just ... fucking fantastic. I feel ... like it's my fucking birthday to celebrate ... even though its not."

"Glad to hear that!" I then asked, "You need a few more minutes to recover from your kinky sex with a blonde blow-up doll?"

Customer number two answered, a lower-pitched voice from the stall, "Yeah, I am still breathing ... hard. Let me catch ... my breath. I will be out of this stall ... within the next few minutes."

"Okay, sounds great!"

Customer number five walked in and said, "I hear you have sexy blow-up dolls." He then asked, "Where are they located?"

I answered, "They are located in each stall."

Customer number five responded, "I can't wait to meet this sexy doll."

Customer number four just left the stall without washing his hands after taking a long shit. I quickly sprayed stall number three to get rid of his strong shit smell.

I responded to customer number five, "There are stalls open, so pick one and enjoy the pleasure moment with the slutty blow-up doll. I just don't understand why guys are so damn turned on with these blow-up dolls when you have so many beauties here at this party."

Customer number five said, laughing, "It's something totally different and discreet."

I responded, "It's not so discreet when you can hear the sex-capades from a previous customer."

"Someone got really too excited and shot his fucking load in her mouth, on her green eyes, and the right side of her face!"

I responded, "Yeah, everyone in this entire men's restroom was aware of his sexual outburst! Everyone in here was rolling their eyes back and looking at each other with a stunned look."

Customer number five said, "What the fuck! He was not shy at all."

I said, "No—not at all, whatsoever."

Customer number five said, "Well, I've got to take a healthy shit. Let me check out number four."

"You got it."

Customer number five just closed the number four stall door.

### 12:10 a.m.

The blow-up doll said, "Hey, gorgeous, you want to play with me? My mouth is wet and ready."

Customer number five, responded, "No wonder guys are getting a fucking hard-on with this sexy, slutty bitch! It fucking talks to you, wants to give you head with its motorized mouth! This fucking doll blows my damn fucking mind!"

"It's been fucking amazing—a one-stop shop for your sexual needs with a discreet quickie behind a closed stall door from a non-human! Wow!"

From stall number four, customer number five said, "Yeah, that was beautifully explained, and yeah, I guess I'm just another male whore! I'm going to be in here for a damn while!"

About twelve minutes later…

The noises said it all—something naughty was happening in stall number four.

### 12:30 a.m.

Customer number five finally came out of the stall and said, "Wow! I needed that quickie. I feel like myself again."

I said with a smile, "I guess now you can enjoy the party with real-life females."

Customer number five, responded, "Yeah, but first I need a good, hard shot of liquor so I can get an amazing fucking buzz!"

"Thank you for the generous tip, and enjoy the party."

Customer number five responded, laughing and relaxed, "The pleasure is mine."

Customers number six and number seven entered the restroom with confused looks.

They both immediately gave me a money tip in my tip jar.

I said with my positive vibe, "Thank you both for the generous tip."

Customer number six said, "My pleasure."

Customer number seven said, "You're very welcome. We heard you have blow-up dolls that need sexual attention. Where are they located?"

I responded, "Yes, above the urinals are your blow-up sheep, and in each stall are your sexy, slutty blow-up dolls."

"Okay, I see the blow-up sheep," said customer number six, looking above the urinals.

Customer number seven said, "I see a sexy blow-up doll in this stall—it's giving me that look that says, 'Here I am. Let's dance and do whatever sexual positions you like.'"

"You will see."

### 12:42 a.m.

Customer number six said to customer number seven, "Let's go into this stall and double team this slutty blow-up doll and shoot our loads all over her fucking face!"

I responded, "Only one human person per stall. Those are the rules of the party. And furthermore, guys, you have top choices here at this party with real-life females."

"We just wanted to score big time with a fucking blow-up doll!"

I said in a firm tone, "You both can go to different stalls!"

Customer number six responded, "I understand."

Customer number seven responded, "Okay."

"Great."

Customer number six said, "I will take stall number one."

"I will take stall number three," replied customer number seven.

"Okay, guys. Please keep your noise down—let's respect other customers who walk into this restroom! Thank you!"

Again, you could hear loud, naughty noises from both stalls. Customer number six was in stall number one, and I could hear his wild sex getting much louder.

**12:50 a.m.**

Customer number six from stall number one said to the blow-up doll, "Yeah, baby, deep throat my cock! That's it, baby! Let me choke your fucking mouth! Yeah, baby, take my hot load! Ahhhhhhhhhhhhhhhhhhhhhhhhhh!"

The blow-up doll said, "Hey gorgeous, you want to play with me? My mouth is wet and ready."

Customer number six responded in a high-pitched voice, "Oh, baby, you want another hot load from my super cock? I have another load to shoot!"

I said loudly, "You did not listen to my earlier instructions about keeping the damn noise down!"

Customer number six walked out of the stall winded and said, "I am so sorry. I just could not stop having so much damn fun with this blonde, slutty blow-up doll. I am leaving the restroom to go flirt with some hot babes."

"Thank you again for the generous tip. Continue with your fun night."

When customer number seven opened stall door number three, he had the eye of a tiger. I said, "Everything okay?"

He said, "Just fine. I took a shit, but I just could not get excited on this brunette, sexy blow-up doll. Honestly, I just did not have the drive to make out with a fucking non-human, blow-up fucking doll. It's just not the real thing. I still can't understand how so many guys back here can manage to get their cum loads off and be extremely proud of it."

"You're the first so far—along with yours truly. Here, let me spray the stall. Okay, let's go to the sink area. Here is foaming soap and a soft-hand towel. Thanks again for your tip."

Customer number seven said, "My pleasure. It's time to check out this wild-ass, fucking party with the real, delicious chicks."

"Have a great time!"

Customers number eight, number nine, number ten, and number eleven walked in wanting to find out about the female blow-up dolls and the blow-up sheep for their erections.

**1:10 a.m.**

Customer number eight said with his exuberance, "Hell, I am looking at this blonde blow-up doll. She has a vibrating motor in her pink pussy and one in her ass! Wonder why the other guys said she only had a motorized mouth?"

Customer number nine responded, "I guess that guy didn't inspect that blow-up doll well enough, or he had a one-track mind for just getting his cock sucked-off!"

I said, "Okay, then, these high-end blow-up dolls is to satisfy you completely on all three of their pleasure holes."

Customer number ten said with a chuckle, "I can see that! I am going into stall number two and fuck this one in her ass, guys. Just give me a few minutes. I will see you out there at the party in a few. Later—it's time to fuck-her-tight-ass!"

Customer number eleven responded, "Well, you know, one of those sheep hanging up there looks really good to fuck!"

I said, "The choice is up to you. There are four blow-up dolls and four blow-up sheep. I'm sure if there was more room in here, we would have more blow-up dolls for a spectacular non-human, high-end blow-up unheard-of-orgy. Wow!"

Customer number eight said, "Yeah, can you imagine? One fucking orgy in this bathroom with all different types of high-end fucking blow-up dolls, and all the real beauties out there at the party going to bed with each other, a lot of incredible licking of their tasty pussies!"

"That thought would just blow my mind, especially with all the fine beauties that are in attendance here at this party. You never know what's going to happen. Never a dull fucking moment, guys! You have enjoyed these high-end blow-up dolls that actually talk to you and fuck like rabbits!"

These wild conversations continued until around 4:30 a.m. The party officially ended at 4:40 a.m. There were a total of about 100 requests for these popular blow-up dolls and blow-up sheep. This prank from the host worked exceptionally well. Only six guys in the men's restroom from the night to the morning hours didn't have sex with one of these non-human dolls. The results were just unbelievable!

Surely, this is a night to always remember.

# Chapter Seventeen
# SEXY AND NAUGHTY!

****

### A night to Remember in Flagler Beach

All of these party nights are so special. There are always so many good laughs from the many hundreds of guests. And, yes, the selected amazing ladies stand out with their sexy and naughty presence. They make sure that their presence is well known throughout each of these so-called naughty, wild parties. This night was no different from the other prestigious party nights of the unknown to those selected few who represent the shining star. It's really fucking remarkable, and just a touch of the tasty icing.

The party started earlier than scheduled thanks to the many outstanding responses from invitations that were sent with a ninety-five percent acceptance. That's so outstanding!

### 6:35 p.m.

Miss Diva Flavor had just finished her exhibition of squatting up and down on a twelve-inch cock stand. A number of observers had cheered her on. This was a sight to see! Now, there was a standing ovation of loud chants, "Miss Diva Flavor, sit on it again and again! We love you!"

And, along with the crowd chanting, big money was thrown in her direction for the hottest performance!

She said, "Now, that's the kinda of workout I love to do, and get generous money from my many amazing fans. And, I feel so damn good about! It's a pick-me-upper like no other!"

Guys were coming into the restroom telling me all about Miss Diva Flavor's performance. It was a party of many highly driven, talented people from all over the world. The main attraction for tonight's entire guest list was a fierce, fun competition. The participant who had the best sex act would be crowned the sexiest, naughtiest, world exhibitionist champion.

**6:45 p.m.**

After several exhibition, live sex shows, Miss Diva Flavor was finally announced the champion. She'd blown her competition away hands down. Back at the men's restroom, several more Miss Diva fans came in.

"What a show, my man!" said a customer who was wearing a Miss Diva Flavor shirt. "The amazing shirt really stands out with a dozen or so bright colors. This shirt has an incredible pic of her fucking her favorite sex stand. She definitely is so fucking amazing!"

Customer number two responded with a grin, "Her knockers and her sweet ass are the best I've ever seen!"

Customer number three said, "She fucked that twelve-inch stand like a pro, and so easily. Her performance and actions were just so brilliant!"

"Wow!"

Customer number four responded with a serious tone, "Whoever fucks her had better keep up with her because she will put a hurting on you really quick!"

Customer number five said, "Making passionate love to Miss Diva would be just a big fucking dream come true!"

"Wow! Keep the confessions coming!"

Customer number six responded, "It would not only be a big dream but also a big feat in the same fucking bed!"

"Wow!"

Customer number seven said with a chuckle, "Being in the same bed with her would keep your horny-self in tiptop shape!" He now entered the stall. "She is sexy and naughty!"

Customer number eight said with a laugh, "Oh, yes, sexy and naughty in the same bed would be sexy and naughty every fucking night!"

"Sounds like a plan!"

Customer number nine responded with a grin, "Knowing that you're getting a piece of ass for the night, you're going to wake up in the morning with the biggest fucking smile!"

"Now we're talking!"

Customer number ten said with exuberance, "You get that piece of ass at night there is a good chance that you wouldn't be horny that next morning! So, in other words, you're not going to be looking for another piece of ass! Boom! There we go! Let's celebrate with joy!"

"That's so right on target! Keep your thoughts coming!"

Customer number eleven responded, "Yeah! That's right! Your cock would be pleased and calm, extremely fucking sensational!"

"Now we're talking! The exciting sex plan of action!"

Customer number twelve said with a big grin, "Sexy and naughty! That's what it's all about! Why the fuck not?"

"That's right! Why not?"

As customer number seven was leaving the stall, he said, "I love these conversations! Sexy and naughty is the way to go! Why not?"

"Why not? Sexy and naughty will fuck your brains right out of your head! 'Oh, baby, be sexy and naughty with me! Place your beautiful breasts all over my face, and I will always tongue your nipples!'"

Customer number thirteen, enjoying a cold beer, slurred with another gulp, "Sexy and naughty. That's where it's at, motherfuckers!"

Customer number fourteen responded, "Hell, yeah! This motherfucker is ready for my sexy and naughty bitch to perform again!"

**7:30 p.m.**

"There is a standing room wait for the famous sexy and naughty. Until next time, guys, another big kinky show by sexy and naughty. Don't miss it. Make sure and mark it on your calendars in two weeks."

The customers remaining in the restroom were exuberant with their high-pitched voices, "Hell, yeah!"

It's time for additional sexy and naughty stories from the new arrivals that have just entered the men's room.

These conversations were so enjoyable and continued to be off-the-fucking wall. Oh, yeah, I want to hear more. Who's next? Just tell me an amazing real-ass confession story. This is the reality, so laugh and laugh again, now your eyes are tearing from so much damn laughter.

# Chapter Eighteen
# SHORT MINI STORIES!

****

**Funny-Ass Confessions in Beautiful Tampa Bay**

Just another day in a men's restroom at a fun sports bar. My presentation was all setup and ready to go. I can't wait for the many exuberant and funny conversations on a busy Friday night. Many hundreds have arrived and are entering one-by-one through the front door for a hot night of fun, and of course to be naughty.

**8:08 p.m.**

A guy went to the urinal, already wasted. He said, slurring, "You know, I just don't know. I am already high. I have been drinking all day. I did walk here because I only live a couple blocks away. Too many shots of whiskey. If I wanted to get a fucking hard-on, it would almost be impossible. I am way, way away from this planet. I see stars in front of me. Yes, I am on another planet. I don't recall the name of the planet that I'm visiting. Could you please tell me what planet I'm on?"

I answered, "Wow, man, you're on planet Earth with all of the Earth people from all over the world. I just don't know anyone on the other planets."

He responded with his slur, "I am looking for Mr. Z, but he doesn't live on planet Earth. I just don't remember what planet he's on."

I said with a laugh, "I have no idea who Mr. Z is. Could he be located on your cell phone favorites?"

The guy answered with total excitement, still slurring his speech, "I think...I remember now. I think he's on planet, My Motherfucking Slut!"

I said with a big laugh, "I never heard of that planet. Wow!" This guy started to walk out of the restroom as he burped and really slurred his voice, "I think I better just chill for a bit."

"Have an amazing night. I do hope that you locate your friend Mr. Z. And, I really don't know what to say about the so-called planet, Your Motherfucking Slut. Take care of yourself."

Wow! Keep having fun with all the funny-ass conversations. It makes the night so damn exciting that you never want to leave this gig.

**10:30 p.m.**

A guy walked into the restroom and started taking a piss in the urinal. He asked, "Do you have cigarettes?"

I answered, "I sure do. Here is my selection of many."

He said, "I think I will take five menthol cigarettes. How much is it?"

I answered, "I will not sell anything off my shelf. It's against the state law since I'm not licensed. I only work for tips!"

He asked, "What is the regular tip per cig?"

"One dollar tip."

"Okay, I will take five of the menthols!" he responded in an exuberant tone.

I said, "Okay, I am going to put four in a box and light the other one for you."

"No, you don't have to do that. Just give me all five."

I received my generous tip. I said, "Thank you."

I handed him five menthol cigs, and then he immediately placed them between his lips.

"Okay, I am ready. Light me up!" he said, chuckling.

"I have never seen anything like this before," I said, laughing. "Mr. Five Cigarette Man, what the hell!"

I lit all five cigarettes for him with my lighter. He was very pleased and smoked all five cigarettes at the same time. We talked and laughed, and I was still extremely surprised.

He said, "This smoke is enjoyable. Thank you for the light."

"My pleasure. What the hell—enjoy your evening, Mr. Five Cigarette Man. We will talk later."

He left the men's restroom still smoking his five menthols at the same time. You had to be there to believe the five-cigarette man. Wow! I'm sure he turned many heads throughout the sports bar.

You never know what's going to take place in a men's restroom.

**11:18 p.m.**

A guy entered the restroom in tears. We greeted each other, and he then went directly to the urinal.

He said, "It's been one of those fucking nights. I came here to have a few drinks to kind of forget about my breakup."

I said, "I'm sorry to hear that. Keep a positive mindset, and always move forward."

He said, "Well, I will be pissing here for a few minutes. I have been drinking a hell of a lot of beer tonight."

"Okay. Take your time. There is no hurry, and no one in line waiting."

The guy said, "Well, my boyfriend broke up with me over two other guys, and a transgender. I miss my gorgeous boyfriend. He used to plow my ass really hard to the point it was sometimes very difficult to get out of bed!"

I responded, "That's way too much information, man. You need to keep your business to yourself and just try to enjoy your night here at this sports bar. I am sure that you will eventually find another guy. This is a diverse nightclub. You will enjoy the clientele here."

He said with a chuckle, "Thank you for giving me advice. I have been loose with my talks at the bar. Oh, shit, everybody at the bar knows now! I really screwed up big time in all of my conversations!"

I said, "You're welcome. Yeah, nobody needs to know that at an open bar. There are things that you say and things you don't say, just chill."

He said with a stern look, "I need to get the fuck out of here, go rest my sore fucking ass, and chill at my apartment. Thank you so much for the foaming soap and towel. I am leaving now."

"My pleasure, and thank you for the generous tip. And, I do hope all goes well for you. Feel better, please take it easy."

It's imperative to have thick skin to be a restroom concierge, as well as having a continuous open mind. Each conversation is totally different, and sometimes they are the unexpected. Again, there's never a dull moment, and definitely have a sense of humor. I just flow smoothly with all the talks.

**12:15 a.m.**

A young man walked into the restroom and headed to the stall and said, "Man, those tacos did a fucking number on me! I just had a couple of beers, and I feel a big shit coming on really quick!"

I responded in a high-pitched voice, "You know, someone earlier commented that the taco dinner didn't agree with him, and he had the runs bad! Hopefully you will feel much better!"

He said in a high-pitched voice, "Oh, shit! It's coming out! Oh, gosh, I have a hell of a lot of shit coming out of my ass! I will be here for a while on this fucking toilet!"

I said with a chuckle, raising my voice just a notch, "Okay, I don't need a play-by-play on your shit session! I am going to spray the bathroom just a bit to calm down the strong smell! Wow!"

The young man said, "That's fine! Yes, my shit is very strong!"

"Okay, well … take your time!"

Another customer headed right to the urinal and said, "Wow! What a motherfucking bad odor in this bathroom!"

"Let me spray the bathroom again to cut some of that nasty smell!"

The young man in the stall yelled, "It's those motherfucking tacos I ate for supper!"

The customer at the urinal asked, "Was it that place two miles down the road heading west?"

The young man answered, "Yes, that's the one!"

The customer said, "Fuck that shit! I won't go there! I don't need the fucking shits all fucking night long! And have that shit smell up my asshole!"

I said with a chuckle, "Then, that settles the taco issue. Boom!"

"He is going to have a raw ass from those fucking tacos!" The customer responded in a firm voice.

The young man said in a high-pitched voice, "Yeah, my ass is very sore— bleeding! And, I need to go home and soak my ass really well in the bathtub with warm salt water!"

"Is it that damn bad? Wow!"

He said, "Yeah!"

I sprayed the bathroom once again. It's a courtesy for everyone who enters the restroom.

### 1:35 a.m.

"Sir, is this the men's restroom?"

I answered, "Yes, it is."

The guy slurred, "I didn't expect a restroom guy to be here. I am just going to use the urinal."

"My name is Dan the Man. I am your restroom concierge."

He paused and slurred, "Look at your amazing fucking presentation. Wow!"

"Thank you so much for your compliment."

He said, slurring, "I am so fucked-up with too many motherfucking shots. My lover is taking my ass home because I can't drive. I'm really fucked-up!"

"Well, that's sensible and the best decision."

He continued to slur, paused, and said, "That's fine, but my lover is a fucking dick! He was hanging all over this guy all fucking night! I really need to spank his motherfucking ass with my leather whips!"

"Well now, it looks like you have a situation, and you know how to resolve it."

He was leaning back and forth at the urinal. He slurred once again as he said, "Yeah, the motherfucker wanted a hot fucking threesome, but I am too fucked-up. Yeah … this piss feels fucking great! I'm in la-la land!"

"Hmm … I don't know what to say."

He left the urinal and said, "I don't want soap. My cock is the cleanest in town!"

I asked, "Not even the hand sanitizer?"

He was really slurring his speech. "No fucking way. My cock is ... my cock, and it's so fucking clean! It's clean ... clean! It's never dirty! I-I ... don't even touch my cock. It springs out of my ... underwear. And, when I'm done pissing, it springs ... automatically back into my underwear. It's the cleanest damn cock in town!"

"Are you sure?" I laughed, hysterically. "Are you bionic?" I continued to laugh and laugh with funny tears from my eyes.

"Fuck, yeah! I just don't have any money to tip you. Sorry, I have to run!"

"Wow! Well, another fictional cock story," I said laughing, continuously.

He immediately wandered off to the patio area of the sports club, now really staggering and shaking a lot of hands. He was having a difficult time walking straight.

Hopefully, these customers who now have his germ, piss cock hands will not rub their eyes. Did I just hear pink eye? Oh, my, now that's a bitch!

### 2:20 a.m.

A customer walked into the men's restroom with a hangover look. His clothes were a bit torn in a number of places, and he had lipstick all over his face and on his neck. Another very interesting scenario.

He said, "I've had an interesting and exciting night!"

"I see."

"She was teasing me all fucking night long, and I had a hard boner to boot!" he said with a goofy look.

"Okay, so, you both didn't decide to have fun in a more private setting?"

He answered, "We could not go to my place—I am married. She could not go to her place because she is married as well."

"I see, so that leaves you ..."

"I'm trying to figure that out. She continued to rub her wet pussy all over my face!" he said.

"Well, now, this is getting to be a very interesting confession."

He then said, "Wow! That piss felt good! Yes, it's driving me fucking crazy. She tastes and smells so fucking good!"

"That would drive me crazy as well. Oh, my!"

He asked, "Any hotels around here?"

I answered, "There are a few down the way. Shouldn't have any problem reserving a room at this time."

He said, "I'll check those out."

"Bye."

### 2:27 a.m.

I heard a voice outside the restroom. A beautiful gal was playing with her breast with one hand and fingering her hot pussy with her other. She said, "I am ready, Honey Macho, let's go find a place, right now!"

He said, "Okay. Let me tip this nice guy. Wait for me outside the club. I will be there in a few minutes."

"Okay, Honey Macho! See you then!"

He washed his hands and dried them with a hand towel. He got a couple of sprays of a great cologne and a couple of breath mints.

I said, "Thank you so much for the generous tip." I then asked, "And, do you mind if I ask you a question, how did you get the name Honey Macho?"

He answered, "Well, she had been rubbing my cock all night, got it really roused, and she called my primary goods Honey Macho."

I laughed and said, "Okay. I believe that you're going to have some fun with your Honey Macho this morning. Enjoy!"

He laughed and said, "Yes, thank you for your amazing customer service!"

"You're welcome. I appreciate all of my customers."

He said, "See you next time."

"It sounds amazing!"

Another guy came in the bathroom and said, "That young lady that was talking to your customer, she actually gives great blow jobs! In other words, she makes her sexy rounds very loosely here at this sports club."

"Wow! I learn something new each night here."

He said, "Yeah, she blew my entire load in my car in the parking lot here about a week ago. She finished, swallowed every bit of it, and then afterwards, my good friend fucked her silly right in my car! She enjoys hot sex in automobiles. It doesn't matter the year and the make of the car."

"Wow! She is really that loose, hmm?" I asked, laughing.

He answered with exuberance, "Hell, yeah! Any time, night or early morning! Another great piss! I feel great now! I've got to continue to go check this sports club out and score big time!"

"Have an amazing morning."

He said, "I plan to. Need to check the hot babes here. I don't have much time before they close. Bye."

"Bye."

Always fun conversations. It's a win-win at these night time, fun-ass, real-life stories.

# Chapter Nineteen
# THIS SIGN REALLY MESSED THEIR MINDS!

****

**A Spectacular Funny-Ass Prank in Tampa Bay**

THE VIP MEN'S ROOM

**No more than one person using this shit stall.
No exceptions. Always be aware of the
unexpected from the ceiling.
Thank you for understanding.**

I created this sign for the stall in the men's room. I am a sense-of-humor guy. And, why not laugh and joke around and from time-to-time play funny pranks. I had no idea that my sign would cause such a shockwave. It has actually messed with the minds of many guys, and there have been so many comments and off-the-wall conversations. I just play along with it, and I sometimes like to play these funny pranks just to see each guy's facial reactions. It's all in fun.

Here are some of the funny-ass conversation pranks from the original times on this easy-going night.

### 9:15 p.m.

Samuel the Prankster, asked, "You want to do it?"

"Yes, let's setup a funny sex prank in the bathroom. Let's get Davion the Great involved again. We can do the same ceiling scenario we did a few months ago. This should be so damn hilarious again. Also, the temporary VIP Men's Room sign will be an eye catcher and mess the minds of many."

"Yeah, Dan, Davion the Great is here. I will be laughing at the bar, drinking my cold beers," said Samuel the Prankster, laughing at these funny-ass pranks.

I said, "Thank you, Samuel the Prankster. Another night of laughter is ahead of us."

Samuel the Prankster responded, "Yeah, my man, laughter keeps you happy. It's always lots of fun."

"Sure does. Laughter is always great and puts a smile on your face."

### 9:55 p.m.

Samuel the Prankster and I greeted each other with our fist bump, and said, "Boom!" Then, our fist bump greeting changed as we immediately opened up the palms of our hands and then our fingers spread quickly in an upward position for our friendly explosion. We then said, "Blow it up!" Now, Samuel went directly to the shitter and closed the stall door.

I asked him in a high-pitched voice, "How has your night been?"

He answered in a high-pitched voice, "It's been fucking amazing, and it's another motherfucking incredible night, so far!"

"That sounds awesome! I see a line is forming outside the restroom!"

After ten minutes . . .

Samuel came out of the stall and said in an exuberant voice, "Dan the Man, this VIP hospitality is fucking amazing! I met Miss G! She came out of the ceiling and gave me a quickie, enjoyed my cock! The sexy baby took my fucking load!"

"That's so awesome! She does give the best head!"

Everyone in line opened their eyes wide during our conversation.

Samuel the Prankster finished drying his hands with a hand towel and smiled. He said, "Thanks so much, my man. I am going back to the bar for some more cold beers! I feel human again!"

"You're welcome. See you later."

The next guy entering the VIP Men's Room said with exuberance, "I can't wait for my hot blow job!"

"Enjoy!"

### 10:15 p.m.

From inside the stall, the guy yelled, "She never came out of the fucking ceiling! My cock is hard, and I'm ready for her!"

In a high-pitched voice, I said, "Well, she might be taking a break! She likes to smoke a cig and have a cold beer to wash down the many hot loads she has taken so far! Give her a few minutes! Just be patient!"

He yelled back, "Okay, but my fucking patience is running thin as a piece of fucking paper!"

I said, "Wow! You don't have much patience at all!"

### 10:22 p.m.

From inside the stall, the guy yelled in an angry tone, "Where in the fuck is this bitch at? I want my fucking blow job, now!"

Once again, in a high-pitched voice, I answered, "Be patient! She likes her cigs and cold beers!"

The guy said in an angry tone, "You mentioned that before! What the hell!"

"Be patient, be cool, and stand by for liftoff!"

He yelled, "What the fuck, man! I am about to just fucking piss on my fucking pants with my hard cock!"

In the meantime, guys in line were getting impatient. For now, only the urinal was in use.

"Man, this is the shit!"

### 10:25 p.m.

Finally, the guy came out of the stall. He was just beside himself. "I fucking can't wait any longer! My wife is at the bar, probably wondering why I took so damn long!"

"Well, now. Keep Miss G a secret."

He said, "Fuck yeah, man! Here's your tip. Later."

"Thank you so much. Cheers."

Then he quickly left the restroom. The next customer arrived in the restroom with the biggest smile.

### 10:30 p.m.

"Dan, how are you?"

I said, "Davion the Great, I am amazing! How's it going?"

"Great, my man!"

He asked, "Is Miss G still around? Is she coming down from the ceiling?"

"Yes, indeed. She was taking a break, but she might be ready for you."

He said, "Can't wait to get my fucking rocks off!"

I said in my exuberant voice, "The stall is all yours, my friend!"

He said, "Thank you, my man. I am going to have my private session of fun!"

The stall was now occupied with Davion the Great. The urinal was in use at this time, and a handful of people in line heard our conversation.

A guy standing in line asked me, "Is it true about Miss G giving head?"

I answered, "It's her specialty, besides other sexual pleasures. She has a beautiful body. As soon as he comes out of the stall, you're next."

"Okay, man. I've got to go. I am just about ready to piss on myself!"

I said, "You don't want to do that. Try to be patient."

"Oh, man, I got to go bad, and now take a mean-ass shit!" he said, holding both legs together. His green eyes showed a look of discomfort.

"That VIP Men's Room sign is blowing me away!" said another customer waiting in line.

### 10:45 p.m.

Davion the Great came out of the stall and said, "She was so fine, and now I have a big-ass smile! I am relieved from all my daily frustrations! I even got to tongue her hard nipples! Wow! She does have a set of enormous fucking knockers! She was upside down from the opening in the ceiling, chained, and, of course, she was eye level to where I was standing, which made it so fucking convenient! She has many sexual tricks! Wow! I am off to the bar again for a celebration drink!"

I responded, "Glad all went well, and enjoy your celebration drink."

The next guy standing in line said, "It's my turn. Here comes that piss, and Miss G, get ready for my horny cock!"

"Just really be patient."

"Hope she is ready and thirsty!" he said, happily.

### 10:55 p.m.

The customer entered the stall with a confident look.

I said, "I will close the stall door."

He said, "Thank you!"

I responded, "My pleasure!"

### 11:02 p.m.

In a high-pitched voice, he asked, "Where is she?"

I answered back, "She's probably taking another break!"

"Shit, man!" He asked again in a high-pitched voice, "Miss G, are you coming down for some sex action? I am ready for you, baby! Please, come down to your daddy!"

A guy pissing in the urinal said in his baritone voice, "Buddy, that ain't going to happen! She's just a fucking made-up imagination! What the fuck!"

He asked with a louder voice from inside the stall, "You mean to tell me she's not real?"

"Dude, get yourself together! No fucking way!"

The guy in the stall asked in a pissed-off voice, "What the fuck is going on?"

The guy pissing finally was now leaving the restroom without washing his hands. He muttered that he had the cleanest hands in town.

I laughed.

**11:07 p.m.**

I then said to the guy inside the stall, "Just hang in there and be patient! I can smell her sensational perfume!"

He said, really angry, "Now, what the fuck is going on? The bitch is not coming out from this fucking ceiling!"

I said, "Just hang in there! I really can smell her sexy perfume!"

He yelled, "Miss G, my cock is hard! I need you, baby, I need you now!"

"That's it, just hang in there! Really hang in there!"

He yelled again, "How long is this going to fucking take, sir?"

"She must be having another cold beer!"

He screamed, "What the fuck! I am losing my fucking patience!"

I asked, "Do you smell that fabulous perfume? Oh, it smells so fine!"

He answered yelling, "What the fuck are you talking about?"

"Her scent smells so fucking good!"

He yelled from the stall once again, "What the fuck is going on! Miss G, you're my bitch! Come out from that motherfucking ceiling, now!"

"Well, well, a little testy, aren't you? Now be nice to Miss G!"

He yelled with his baritone voice, "This bitch is playing a fucking mind game! I am going fucking crazy! I am in no fucking mood for these shitty-ass motherfucking games!"

"Be calm! Take a deep breath and be confident!" I said, exuberantly.

He asked in his angry tone, "Where in the fuck is she? What the fuck is going on? She is really taking a long motherfucking break!"

"Just hang in there! Be patient! She loves her cigs and cold beer!"

He belted from the stall, "No shit, man, she must be taking a fucking long nap, and her fucking dreams are taking her to another fucking planet!"

"She tends sometimes to take long-ass naps! Just be patient!"

### 11:15 p.m.

The stall door opened quickly. He had a pissed-off, intense look on his face. It was bright red, and he was dripping wet from his sweat. He ended up getting one hell of workout as he worked himself into a wild-ass frenzy.

"This must be a motherfucking scam!" he said, angrily.

Samuel the Prankster walked in and headed to the stall. He asked, "What's going on?"

I answered, "This gentleman wants to know the whereabouts of Miss G."

Samuel the Prankster said, "Well she gave me a great blow job earlier, and then she ended up taking a long smoke and a cold beer break."

I said, "He thinks that this is a scam."

Samuel the Prankster said, "Oh, hell, no! Patience is the name of this fucking sex pleasure!"

"What the fuck!"

I said, "See? Be patient."

"I'm leaving! I had enough of this motherfucking bullshit!"

He left the restroom steaming and so pissed.

### 11:20 p.m.

"Well, Dan, we pulled another funny-ass prank," Samuel the Prankster said, laughing.

I was really laughing and said, "That guy was all twisted and fired up—he was really extremely mad! Our game plan was to play a prank, not to get anyone that fucking pissed!"

Samuel, the Prankster responded, "Yeah, I know, Dan."

### 11:22 p.m.

Now, Davion the Great entered the restroom, laughing.

Davion the Great said, "Dan the Man and Samuel the Prankster, that guy was so fucking pissed at the bar! He was telling people how his so-called ceiling date fucked him over big time! The people at the bar just had a stunned look and were rolling their eyes!"

"Wow! He was beside himself. It was not our plan to get anyone mad. We just wanted to play a funny prank," I said, laughing with funny tears in my eyes.

Samuel the Prankster said, "He will never forget this episode."

I said, "I'm sure he will not. I do hope he settles down, and he has a good time. Well, guys, until next time, same time, same location, and same restroom, enjoy the rest of your club hours."

"See you. Hope the rest of the club night is a spectacular one, Dan the Man!" Samuel the Prankster said, laughing.

"Until next time, my man, Dan the Man," Davion the Great said, laughing with his big-ass sparkling diamond grills.

"Bye, guys," I responded, still laughing.

Until next time for another funny prank in the VIP Men's Room.

## Chapter Twenty
# LET'S PLAY WORD-FOR-WORD!

****

### A Wild-Ass Night in Winter Park

I had just finished setting up my presentation display in the men's guest party bathroom. The host was expecting another huge party in his exclusive, fun mansion with his many acres of land filled exotic animals for everyone to see and photograph. Their pics would be unbelievable! This was a wild and crazy-ass site with many of the strangest sounds that you could ever imagine.

My regular customer came into the men's restroom. His name was BX, a retired stock market analyst, and he was always popular at these elite parties. He was ready to play another word-for-word game with me. The game includes all alphabet letters and words. The rules of the word-for-word game is to have an acceptable match for a given word, or even a given word that rhymes with another given word or even complete a two word short phrase. For example, the word time would be acceptable for the word watch. Another example, the letter I would be acceptable for the word won, which then "I won" completes the two word short phrase. The third example, the word lotion would be acceptable for the word massage. The first player to answer with the word won two consecutive times will win the word-for-word game. It's always fun when your opponent is really lit.

## 10:35 p.m.

BX mentioned he had downed fifteen shots at the bar and received an amazing blow job from a hot dancer here at this party. Well, it was time to get started with another word-for-word game, with the opponent starting to feel his space flight going into outer space.

BX asked, "Dan the fucking Man, are you ready to play, my man? Oh, bye the way, this seating area in this luxury bathroom is fucking amazing!"

I answered, "Let's go, BX! Yes, it is! And, Candy will serve your drinks."

Candy said, "Pleasure to meet you, BX."

BX said, "Candy, the pleasure is mine."

I said, "Okay, we can officially begin the game."

BX started the game by saying, "Hole."

I said, "Ass."

BX said, "Cunt."

I responded, "You're so damn bad! The c-word. Whoa! Well, I am going to say ... the word pussy."

BX said, "Tongue."

I said, "Lick."

BX said, "Suck. Wait, Dan, I need to have my shot of tequila. Oh, my, I am kicking now!"

I said, "Fuck."

BX said, "Anal."

I said, "Ass."

BX said, "Fuck."

I said, "Suck."

BX slurred, "Eat."

I said, "Pussy."

BX slurred, "Lick."

I said, "Pussy."

BX slurred, "Ass."

I said, "Hole."

BX slurred, "Tasty."

I said, "Pussy."

BX slurred, "Fuck."

I said, "Pussy."

BX slurred, "Anal."
I said, "Sex."
BX slurred, "Tongue."
I said, "Tits."
BX slurred, "Nipples. Wait, Dano. Just got another shot of tequila from Candy. Oh, shit, that's so fucking great! Oh, fuck, yeah, my man!"
I said, "Hard."
BX slurred, "Blow."
I said, "Jobs."
BX slurred, "Pussy."
I said, "Eat."
BX slurred, "Cock."
I said, "Lover."
BX slurred, "Hmm … my secret … um … mistress!"
I said, "Wow!"
BX slurred, "Whoa!"
I said, "Beauties!"
BX slurred and asked, "What the … okay … what the … fuck?"
I answered, "Fucker."
BX slurred, "Mother."
I said, "Fucker."
BX asked, "What the … duck?"
I answered, "Fuck."
BX asked, "What the … fuck is … this? Is this … hot?"
I answered, "Sex."
BX slurred, "My … hmm … mistresses!"
I said, "Lovers!"
BX asked, "What's up … player?"
I answered, "Game."
BX paused and asked slurring, "What fucking … game? Wait a fucking minute, Dano … another shot has arrived from Candy!"
I answered, "Player."
BX slurred, paused and asked, "What … what?"
I answered, "Sweet."
BX paused and slurred asking, "For …
what the … fuck … is that?" I answered, "Suck."

BX paused and said, "I am ... fucked. Playing!"
I said, "Game."
BX asked, "Wha ...?" He paused again,
and said, "What game?" I answered, "Chess."
BX slurred and asked, "What ... che-ss-chess?"
I answered, "Checkmate!"
BX slurred, "I-I ... I ..."
I said, "Won."
BX slurred and asked, "You ... did ... what ... the ...I?"
I answered, "Won!"
BX slurred, "I ... what ... the ... fuck!"
I said, "BX, my friend, the game is over!"
BX slurred and asked, "Wha-what?"
I answered, "Game over. I won, BX!"
BX slurred and waved to Candy at the front door, "Honey ... bring ... me ... another ... drink ... drink ... dri ... anoth ... err ... sh-shot!"

BX has been a fantastic customer for the past several years. He loves playing the word-for-word game at these elite parties.

As he has stated so many times, "It's ... a ... amazing, fucking ... bla ... st!"

And, my response has always been, "I know. Just hang in there, my friend! It's always my pleasure, and, of course, a hell of a lot of fun!"

Yes, this mansion party was about to explode with hundreds and hundreds of famous people. It would be another blast, with many more word-for-word games in the men's restroom. It's all in fun.

**11:10 p.m.**

TM walked into the bathroom and said, "Great to see you again, Dan. I heard you're the champion of the word-for-word game!"

I said, "Great to see you as well, TM. I don't know about that, but I really enjoy playing the game. It's a fucking blast!"

He said, "Well, I had a few shots already. I need to down a few more, and then I will come back and we will play an exciting word-for-word game, my fucking man!"

"Okay, TM, sounds great. Enjoy your shots at the bar. I'll be here and ready."

He left the restroom to the open bar area for some more tasty shots.

**11:20 p.m.**

After he left, I murmured, "Another win coming up, and another interesting round."

The guy at the urinal said, "Dan, you will always do well playing this bathroom game. The guys are drunk, and you remain sober during your gig."

"I keep it professional, as always."

He said, "Advantage goes to Dan. The disadvantage goes to the clients who are totally lit!"

I said, "I have to admit that it's fun, funny, and a fucking blast!"

He said, "I know, my man. You're great to be here at these elite parties. We appreciate you. Later."

"Thanks. Have an amazing time. Cheers!"

It's all in fun having an incredible blast.

# Chapter Twenty One
# NEVER DULL MOMENTS AT THE URINAL!

****

**A Laid-Back Fun Night of Laughter in Tampa**

There are never dull moments in a men's restroom. Each night is totally different than the night before, including all the funny-ass conversations. At the urinals, as guys piss, they sometimes vent what's on their minds, tell their many stories, and then they leave the restroom. Then, the next ones do it all over again. So many fucking confessions at each urinal.

**10:50 p.m.**

A guy entered the restroom and went directly to the urinal. "Oh, man, I have to take a piss really bad!"

"Okay." Then I asked, "How has your night been?"

He answered, "It was going great. This good-looking bitch wanted to suck my dick in my car, but her girlfriend talked her out of it."

"That's a tough break."

He said, "Tell me about it. Her girlfriend wants to eat her pussy so bad, and I tried to pursue a fun threesome, but it did not fall in my direction. I mean, I told her, 'While your girlfriend is eating your beautiful, tasty pussy, you can give me head, and I can play with your beautiful tits!'"

"Wow, that's exciting!"

"Her expression told me that her girlfriend is definitely in the way. She does not want to be involved in a hot threesome," he said.

I said, "Well, that's a real shame. Though, the night is still young."

He responded, "Yeah, I know. I got to release my power milk load very soon before I fucking drown in it!"

I said, "You know, there are a lot of young ladies out tonight."

He said with a grin, "Yeah, they are out tonight, big time!"

"Well, you never know from one minute to the next who's ready for a party of hot sex."

He responded, "Yeah, I am going to cruise around the club and see if getting laid tonight is a possibility!"

"Have fun with your sexy sight-seeing."

He responded, "I needed that encouragement!"

"It's my pleasure."

"Bye."

"Cheers."

**11:15 p.m.**

A new customer arrived, now standing at the urinal. "This piss feels really good. I was ready to piss on myself!"

"There was one guy earlier who pissed in his pants. His girlfriend was so furious at him. She was livid as hell!"

He said with a concerned look, "I have an odd situation tonight."

"Really? What's your confession?"

"I have my wife here—and two girlfriends," he answered, chuckling.

"Oh, my. That's not only odd, it could be fucking dangerous!"

He said, "Yeah, Dan, I got myself in a fucking hell of a bind tonight. Even though they are not drinking together, they all know each other. All three are just incredible in bed. They give me consistent, hot, hot lovemaking, and they taste so fine!"

"Wow!" I then asked, "What the hell are you going to do?"

He answered, "I have no fucking idea, but I'd better think of something quickly."

"Yeah, I'm afraid so."

He said, "If only I could disappear, like being beamed up to another location far, far away."

### 11:25 p.m.

He got his hands washed with foaming soap I placed on the palms of his hands, and he enjoyed the service experience with a soft-hand towel. I chuckled and said, "You have been watching too many of those sci-fi programs."

He said, laughing, "It's my sense of humor, but yeah, this isn't a television show."

I laughed and said, "No, it's sure as hell isn't."

He said, "I am going through that door to escape for now and gather my fucking thoughts!"

"Well, take care, but you know you have to come up with a solution. You can't hide forever. Then all three are going to say, 'Come out, and come out, wherever you are.'"

He said in a firm tone, "Oh, gosh, I know! Talk later, Dan."

"Yes, talk later, and I hope the best for you."

He quickly said, "Bye, my friend."

"Bye."

He scrammed out, opened the bathroom door and disappeared quickly. Outside, I could hear the song of a famous Motown artist playing with a soothing sound and great positive vibes. Oh, yes, just an amazing song.

### 11:35 p.m.

"I just don't know what I am going to do these days!" A new customer said in a serious tone while pissing in the urinal.

I asked, "Is everything okay?"

He answered with his frown expression, "Well, I know I've had a few too many shots tonight. My boyfriend cheated on me last night with another guy and another gal. We are bisexual."

"Hmm, I did not need to know your sexual preference. That's way too damn much information. So . . . okay, how do you feel about this situation?"

He answered, "It really sucks! I thought we had a great thing at our house, the three of us!"

"Okay. The three of you?"

He said with a big smile, "Two guys and a gorgeous gal. All three of us have fun with our sexual desires and fantasies."

"Okay."

**11:42 p.m.**

He washed his hands with foaming soap and got a nice, soft-hand towel to dry his hands. He said, "I really appreciate your customer service!"

"Thank you."

He responded, "You're welcome."

I asked, "So going back to our original conversation. I heard your confession, and my question to you is why did he break loose for another sexual encounter?"

He answered, "He wanted to fuck me in my ass, and I wasn't in the mood to get fucked that early in the morning!"

"Oh . . . Hmm."

He said, "I am still walking around with a very sore ass from the night before!"

"This is really some confession. So . . . you have sex every day?"

He answered quickly, "Almost every day."

I asked, "How does the gorgeous gal feel about these sex thrills every day?"

He answered, "She loves the excitement every night. She is a nympho—has to have sex every day."

"That's very interesting." I asked, "What does she love to do?"

He answered with a grin, "While my boyfriend is fucking my asshole, I fuck her in her amazing wet pussy!"

"Whoa, okay! This is some kinky, off-the-wall confession! Does she like to do any other positions?"

He answered, "We have a leather sling. She loves to lie on it with her hands tied to the back of the hang-up chains and her legs tied in an upward position on the front hang-up chains. Then we take turns. She loves to suck cock, drain it completely, and get fucked at the same time!"

"Wow, what a hot confession."

He said, "There is a hell of a lot of hot sex in our house! It never stops!"

I said, "These are some kind of confessions."

He said, "Oh, hell, yeah! I have a lot more, and we have many more sexual positions!"

"I'm sure you do. And, some you don't want to say."

He responded, "Not really. We have an open agenda. We all want to make sure that each one of us is extremely happy with our sex drives and our fantasies!"

"But there is a missing piece to this conversation."

He had a puzzled look and asked, "What is missing?"

My answer was to the point, "She has to have a female sex friend, a girlfriend. Is this correct?"

He answered with a surprise look, "Oh, wow, you nailed it! She sure does. Her lover comes over once in a while, and she and her girlfriend make passionate love for many hours, and their pussies together are just so fucking incredible! Their pussy juice together makes a powerful energy drink!"

"I'm sure it does. It would do very well in a sex-specialty market."

He said, "I can't say, but it would sure turn heads! Pussy juice at its finest and tastes so damn great!"

I asked, "Has it come to all four of you having wild sex at the same time?"

He answered, "Great question. We have sure thought about it. In time, I'm sure it will take place, and it will be a wild-ass party of hot, steamy sex!"

"Wow!"

He said with exuberance, "Let me backtrack that statement. The foursome might happen sooner. Her girlfriend did play with her tits and tongued them in front of me the other day. It was so fucking amazing!"

I responded with a chuckle, "That's very nice, man. It may be sooner than what you expected. That's great excitement!"

"You just get so fucking excited with that fine pussy!"

I said with a grin, "Yes, you will. It's what keeps us feeling so damn fucking amazing, and we have the biggest smiles on our faces!"

He said, "Man, does it ever. I have the best of both worlds!"

"I see that you're happy."

He responded, "Oh, fuck, yeah! Happy as a clam."

Laughing, I said, "Okay."

Laughing, he said, "Hey, I got to go."

"Have an amazing night," I said, laughing.

"Catch you later!"

"Cheers."

**12:15 a.m.**

A guy walked up to the urinal and said, "I got to piss with a hard-on. I may be taking a little longer than most."

I said, "Take your time. I don't have a stopwatch."

He said, "I just fucked this bitch in the alley in the back of this club, and now I am fucking hard again!"

"Wow! I guess that's a good thing."

He responded with a grin, "I just need to relax a bit and enjoy some fucking shots of liquor over at the far bar. The bartender there has some really big tits, some of them hanging out of her slutty, tight-ass blouse!"

"Yeah, the customers here do mention her a lot with their tongues hanging out."

He responded with laughter, "I would love to tongue her tits right at her bar!"

"Well, a lot of guys would love to do that same thing," I said with a grin.

He said, "I guess I am going to be horny all fucking night long with her sexy presence at the bar!"

"I am sure a lot of guys will be in the same situation. Though, that's a positive."

He said, "Let me go check her out in person and have some really stiff shots. Later, my man."

"Later. Do have an amazing time."

"Later."

## 12:45 a.m.

A guy pissing in the urinal asked with a slur, "What the fuck? Where am I?"

I chuckled and answered, "You're at a nightclub."

He said slurring, "On a fucking Monday night? What the fuck!"

"Monday night."

He said, slurring, "Okay, Monday night. I don't fucking believe it!"

"Yes, do believe it."

"What the fuck?" he asked slurring, with a stern look.

"You know where you're at now?"

He asked, "What city is this?"

"Here in beautiful Tampa!"

He slurred, paused once again, and asked, "What … the … fuck … is?"

"I do not understand your question."

"Is this planet Earth … or … damn … what?" he asked, really slurring, pausing, and drooling at the same time.

I answered, "This is our planet Earth."

He slurred, burped his beer, and asked, "How can I … get to the next … planet … over?"

I answered, laughing, "Simple—a spaceship."

"Fuck, man!" he said, and burped a few more times. He then asked, "How do I … get one of those … spaceships?"

I answered, "I believe that you have to be an astronaut to qualify for a space flight to the next planet, if that's where they're going."

He said, slurring, "What the fuck … I thought … I can get into a spacecraft … and fly."

"No, I believe it doesn't work that way at all."

"I need another … fucking shot … of straight … liquor!" he slurred and burped several times, then asked, "Will you … be my driver … in … the morning?"

"No, I am not the driver. I am your restroom concierge."

He slurred and said, "That really … sucks. Fucking, shit, man!"

"Your drivers are in the front of the club. Any one of them would be glad to take you directly to your residence. Of course, for a fee."

He once again slurred his speech, burped his beer and said, "I am going to take another sip … of my cold beer. I can't … drive. I … am so fucked-up. I-I-I … need a … driver!"

"No problem. I will send him a text immediately. Okay. Done. He will arrive here in the bathroom within the next two minutes."

"That's fucking … quick, my man!" he slurred and burped again. He then asked, "Do I … have time … to get some slutty … bitch to take home? I need a … fucking … blow job … really … bad!"

I answered, "There is no time at all. Here is your driver." He slurred to the driver, "Mr. Driver, I am … fucked … up. Take me to … my home. I still … don't know … what planet … I'm on?"

The driver answered, "This planet has so many stories. Sir, you made a wise choice to be driven instead of actually trying to drive in your condition!"

He asked, "Do … you have … any pussy … in your … car?"

"No sir, I do not. Why don't we walk to my car? It's not far from here."

"Okay, my fucking … dude," he said, slurring and sipping his cold beer.

I said, "Guys, have a wonderful morning!"

The driver said, "Thank you, Dan."

I said, "You're welcome, Sam the Enforcer."

Sam and the customer left. No doubt, this customer needed help and in no way could even have attempted to drive his own car. As funny as this was at the time, doing a good deed for your customer is always a good thing.

## Chapter Twenty Two
# A WILD, UNUSUAL ALUMNI PARTY!

****

### A Fun Blast, but a Painful Night in Gainesville

It was time for another alumni party in a town that loves to drink and celebrate all kinds of special occasions. The party atmosphere is always here and never sleeps with total exuberance.

"It's just a wild-ass fucking alumni party to never forget!" said a spokesperson on the alumni committee. It was held in a rented activity center with two thousand invited guests, and hundreds of hot strippers for entertainment who were kinky as hell. There was also a beautiful buffet of tasty food, and yours truly in charge of the men's restroom number two with an amazing presentation, and ready to provide compassionate customer service.

### 11:00 p.m.

"Its show time, everyone!" The host said at the podium on the main floor. He received a standing ovation from all the happy guests.

The alumni party officially began with complimentary drinks at the seven big bars. The bars were filling fast, and the bartenders were making drinks as quickly as possible. It was the start of a wild and crazy-ass night.

And, back at my assigned restroom …

## 11:10 p.m.

Customer number one entered the bathroom and said, "Tonight is a night of celebration. I'm going to get fucked-up and get laid with these gorgeous bitches!"

I responded, "This should be a dandy of an alumni party." Customer number one said, "This is a fucking crazy-ass alumni group. These people are from all over the country."

"Glad we have the additional security present."

Customer number one responded, "Yeah, they will need the extra security with those fucking muscles!"

"I am never concerned about having security around. Matter of fact, we need security to be safe."

Customer number two entered the bathroom and said, "These strippers are all walking around wearing only skimpy thongs, and their boobs are nude as fuck. They are all flashing their hard, tasty nipples!"

"Wow!" I responded with a chuckle. "This party will be semi-nude at the beginning, and then I believe it's going to be all nude very soon."

Customer number three said, "I am really feeling good after my blow job in the kitchen from this gorgeous chick. It was so fucking amazing, and she swallowed my entire load!"

I said, "Well, so the kitchen now becomes a different place for hot sex—wow, what a hot confession."

Customer number three responded, "Yeah, I sat on a small corner counter, and she went to town on my hard cock, then, when she drained me, she topped it off with a cold beer. The cook was nearby making some food on the hot stove."

"I'm sure she enjoyed that with a cold beer."

Customer number three said with his chuckle, "Yeah, she sure did—she was so damn thirsty!"

"Wow."

Customer number three said, "I am craving some more hot sex. I am going to check out some of these rich bitches!"

### 11:35 p.m.

"This is the top-of-the-line selection of sluts for every single guy here."

Customer number three responded, "Yeah, I am going back to the party. Later, my man."

I responded with a chuckle, "It sounds great. Later."

Customer number four walked in with a smile on his face. "I just got a special treat in a storage room, and I am on cloud nine, just sizzling!"

I said, "Wow. What was your special treat?"

He answered, "The slut gave me an outstanding blow job, and at the same time, her blonde friend was fucking my ass with a strap-on pleasure cock. Then, when I shot my load, they both took every tasty drop of it!"

I laughed and said, "Wow! That's truly a different sex scenario. Are you happy with the sexual outcome?"

Customer number four answered with exuberance, "Hell, yeah! I am so fucking happy, and it did relieve all of my fucking stress!"

I said, laughing, "Wow! It's really nice to see that you have the biggest smile."

He said, "I am beside myself. The hot, kinky sex was so sensational—it felt like no other! I feel so damn amazing … like I am on top of the world, like a champion!"

"Wow! Your words are just so incredible."

Customer number four said, "I am going back for some more kinky sex. Later."

"Do enjoy, and have fun with your kinky, stress-relieving sex," I said, laughing.

### 11:45 p.m.

Customers number five, six, seven, eight, nine, and ten arrived in the restroom with happy faces.

I said, "Happy night, guys!"

They burst out laughing. One customer said, "We just had kinky sex with some fine-ass bitches!"

I said, "This party is starting to get wild." I then asked, "When you say kinky, are there some specifics on the type of sex you were looking for?"

"We got our cocks sucked and asses fucked at the same time. We enjoy this type of kinky fucking, hard-driving sex! Now we feel so damn amazing! We are lit as fuck, motherfuckers rolling on easy street, heading to our motherfucking golden paradise!"

"Okay, wow! That's some confession."

**11:55 p.m.**

Customer number eleven arrived limping into the restroom, and his face was showing some discomfort.

"Wow! A hell of a way to explain this one! The guy who was here using the restroom just a few minutes ago was explaining his kinky sex experience as well. He was feeling so damn sensational! He had the biggest smile that I have ever seen at one of these parties!"

Customer number eleven said, "Yeah, I got my cock sucked by a beautiful blonde and another blonde fucked me so hard with her strap-on! My ass is so damn sore! She did a fucking number on my asshole!"

I responded, laughing, "These confessions are the trend of the party—two gals to every guy. You get your dick sucked, but you're bent over because they want to plow your ass with a strap-on!"

Customer number eleven responded, "Yeah, man, I would say that my confession is that . . . that's the reality of this fucking party! The alumni brats are enjoying their blow jobs and getting their motherfucking asses pounded!"

"I have never heard before these unusual confessions in the men's restroom!" I then asked, "There is a missing piece of this scenario. What is missing here that I should know about?"

Customer number eleven said with his grin, "This was a planned revenge party on these brats because of a recent gang bang party they hosted. It turned out so fucking bad! It's going to get even fucking wilder as the night goes on and will extend to the early-morning vampire revenge hours!"

I asked with a surprise look, "How much wilder can it fucking get?"

He answered, "The party is still young, and these ladies are ready to rumble all fucking party long with their revenge in sight. They are doing some heavy lines."

I murmured, "I see. Another crazy confession. This party is a book in itself."

Customer number eleven said, laughing, "I will read it and laugh my motherfucking ass-off!"

"I always laugh at every one of these wild-ass parties that continue to have so many unexpected surprises! It sure as fuck makes for an amazing book to read and enjoy with a good stiff drink beside you!"

These guys were once again getting hammered so fucking bad, walking around with sore asses, and getting so fucked-up on an enormous display of a beautiful fountain of champagne. Wow! It was still early at this party. I was waiting for more of the unexpected.

### 1:30 a.m.

I had now had conversations in the men's restroom with about 150 guys who had been so stone drunk with many glasses of champagne, flipped over in different positions, and now had sore asses from strap-on cocks. They'd had their cocks sucked and completely drained from many fine females, and they really didn't know where in the hell they were at. It was the biggest surprise at this stunning party.

The morning hours were dazzling, and another customer entered the restroom, exhausted. He said, "I was involved in an amazing threesome. I need to just take a breather. It was the hottest sex bang I've ever been in!"

I said, "I have definitely heard a hell of a lot of real confessions from your co-workers during the course of this unusual alumni party. Let me guess—do you have a sore ass?"

He said, "Oh, no. It wasn't like that. I teamed up with another guy, and we gang banged this chick silly as fuck! I had my cock in her ass, and my buddy had his cock in her pretty pussy. We were going to town, and she was so excited about our fucking. She told both of us, 'Don't stop, my hot-as-fuck cock motherfuckers! It feels so fucking amazing! Keep fucking me! I love every fucking minute of it!'"

I said, chuckling, "All right. Well, now, this sex encounter was totally different from the other hundred and fifty or so guys who were pounded in their asses!" I then asked, "How did everything turn out after it was all done?"

He answered, laughing, "We could not have stopped because we were fucking in overdrive. She received two hot loads inside of her, and she took every bit of it with the biggest fucking smile."

"What a hot confession. No wonder you're so damn worn out!"

### 2:30 a.m.

I would say going by my hand towel count, that number 175 had just entered with his tongue hanging out, catching his breath, and a bath towel covering his privates. He now has a confession.

He said, "I am a tiny bit exhausted. There were two of us switching-off on the sex slings and having some erotic sex. I mean some hard ass-fucking. Both gals were semi-nude with their sexy-as-hell fucking lace stockings and their sexy pumps. We tied them to the leather slings. They lay on their backs with their legs tied up, and our fucking cocks never stopped. And, we kept switching chicks. It was so damn cool, with a hell of a lot of whipped cream and warm oils."

"Wow! That was some erotic sex blast, with the oils and whipped cream!"

He said, "To top it off, afterwards, these two chicks made passionate love together with both of our loads inside their pretty pussies! They went to town, eating each other out, their hot, wicked tongues digging down and tasting our loads of crème delights!"

I said, "Now, this is a wild sex confession. Wow!"

He said, "Yeah, it doesn't get any better than that."

"It sure doesn't. Here is another wow! There are still so many real sex confessions to hear."

He asked, "Well, do you have a pad of a hundred pages or so?"

I answered, "Okay, we can meet for coffee one morning. This will be just amazing. I can sort through them for the funniest, hottest, and naughtiest for my future books. I am looking forward to more real, naughty stories."

We exchanged business cards, and I scored an important coffee get-together.

"JoJo, it was a great pleasure communicating with you."

He responded, "Hell, yes! I will definitely promote your books on my social media."

"I really appreciate that, JoJo. Thank you so much."

"My pleasure, Dan the Man. You're so fucking real and awesome," he said, laughing.

"You're so damn cool," I said with my Dan the Man smile of compassion, pride, and dignity.

"Cheers, my man of the fucking hour!" he said, exuberantly.

"Cheers!"

# The Cast

Dan the Man
Mr. Rymo the Lover
Jack the Pirate
Dyno the Twist
Miss Sluthole the Queen
Mr. Fucker
Mr. Muscles
Mr. Cool the Winner
Mr. Q
JJ, Mr. Lick Man
Mr. Shit Hands Man
Mr. D the Smooth Man
Mr. Freak
Mr. B
Miss Bango
Paramedic Team
DJ XO
Kinky Man
Sunshine
Mr. M the Hip Man
Miss Z Sexy Babe
Dick the Snake
Mr. Malto the Magician

Honey Bunny
Mo the Slammer
PJ the Jock
Jason Dillard
Mr. Dom Freakinghowser
The Motorized Blow-up Dolls
Blow-up Sheep
Pitcher Beer Man
Miss Diva Flavor
Ali-Mo
Mr. Z Man
Mr. Five Cigarette Man
Honey Macho
Samuel the Prankster
Miss G
Davion the Great
BX
TM
Candy
Sam the Enforcer
The Alumni Brats
Strap-On Ladies
JoJo

*Author Head Shot Photo by Joshua J. Stringer, Instagram @rastarabbi, www.sofloentrepreneur.com*

# Appreciation Quotes

*If you break the seal, you have to learn to have a good time in the restroom, and there is no better time than time with Dan the Man!*

—Ian Urie, Brandon, Florida

*Dan the Man—he is so damn cool and smooth, and he has the right mindset for this profession!*

—Jay Cambridge, Clearwater Beach, Florida

*Dan the Man is the best restroom concierge in the entire fucking world!*

—Bernie L, Simms, Houston, Texas

*You know, I can be not up to par, just having one of those days. Then, I start talking to Dan the Man. He really puts a smile on my face, and then I am a happy camper!*

—Joe Silverstien, Atlantic City, New Jersey

*Dan the Man is the fucking bomb! He communicates to me like my loving family does!*

—M.J. Johnson, Atlanta, GA

*Dan the Man, you treat everyone the same. I love that about you!*

—L.J. Soto, Miami, Florida

## DAN THE MAN

*I have a new family member, and his name is Dan the Fucking Man! He is the best restroom guy in the USA!*

—A.J. McCathy, Orlando, Florida

*Dan doesn't just run the bathroom—he runs a venue. Whether you're knee-deep in shit or just need to shit, he knows the right vibe!*

—Joe Galatie, Tampa, Florida

*He runs a men's bathroom like a five-star hotel. He is the best at what he does. Dan is the coolest, with a positive vibe of excellence!*

—Tom Bridge, Ft. Lauderdale, Florida

*I can't wait until his second book is published. I want to laugh my ass-off with some cold beers. Oh, hell, yes!*

—Jimmy T. Malto, Bronx, New York

*Dan the fucking Man, that is who he is. He is so upbeat! It makes you love him like your own brother! Wow!*

—Tony C. LaBlanco, Queens, New York

*Dan the Man—he is the man of the hour. He fires me up like a firecracker that just popped!*

—Tim Bryant, St. Louis, Missouri

*Dan the Man, that says it all—number one in the world!*

—John Michael Luciano, New York City, New York

*Bravo, Dan the Man, again, Bravo Danielson!*

—Joe Leo, San Francisco, California

*Dan the Man—he's the fucking man with a plan of exuberance! He makes me laugh, he makes me smile. We have great conversations. He's so compassionate, and he is the real deal—nothing fake about this old-timer!*

—Jack Becket, Winter Park, Florida

# Let's Talk

**Instagram**
teamdantheman1

**Facebook**
Daniel Hernandez

**LinkedIn**
teamdantheman

**Company Website**
www.teamdantheman.com

# My Daily Poem

Start the day, thank you God,
say prayers and be so blessed.
Kiss my baby, cherish the day.
Chill, communicate, and focus.
Keep a positive, sound mindset.
Working out, it's so motivating.
Set goals, avoid the negativity.
Writing a manuscript, laugh.
Keep reaching, the bright star.
Have the vibe, it's so beautiful.
Stay in the moment, it's amazing.
Keep a winning attitude, it's lit.
The day is amazing, enjoy success.
Never give up, great things come.
Have faith, always with passion.
It's a great feeling, having power.
Rewards come, but have a plan.
Never stop, you have confidence.
Keep the positive, spirits are high.
I am so happy, keep having fun.
Now, time to relax, chill again.
Let's talk, love you my life love.
Time again, pray and be blessed,
thank you God for another day,
having you daily is incredible.
My love, time to enjoy together,
love you, a compassionate heart.
Catch up, truly another positive.
Now, another day ends, kiss you,
sweet dreams, another good night.
Life is always amazing; live life,
be grateful, sincere and be you.

*Love, Hugs, Peace, and God Bless,*

*Dan the Man*

# About the Author

Dan the Man is exuberant with a positive mind-set. He was born and raised in Ybor City, the historic district of Tampa, Florida. He has been married to his beautiful wife, Joni, for nearly four decades. He is proud of his entire talented family and their two fun, amazing cats.

Dan earned a Bachelor of Science in Business Management and a Master of Arts in Organizational Management from the University of Phoenix.

He states, "I enjoy writing nonfiction, reality. I am amazed that no one has ever written about these real confessions in a men's restroom. I get to eavesdrop on naughty confessions, which give us all many laughs."

Dan continues writing additional naughty confessions and has begun another funny manuscript for future publication. He has hundreds of real stories to share with the entire world.

www.ingramcontent.com/pod-product-compliance
Lightning Source LLC
LaVergne TN
LVHW091555060526
838200LV00036B/852